The Mary of the Celts

The Mary of the Celts

Andrew Breeze

GRACEWING

First published in 2008

Gracewing
2 Southern Avenue
Leominster
Herefordshire HR6 0QF

ISBN 978 0 85244 682 9

Typeset by Action Publishing Technology Ltd,
Gloucester GL1 5SR

Contents

Preface

The Mary of the Celts brings together papers published between 1983 and 1999 in British, Irish, French, and Canadian journals, and I thank their editors for permission to reprint. However, in presenting the material as a whole I have made hundreds of minor changes. Most of these are stylistic and concern the text, but I have also pruned references to keep the bibliography within limits. For detail on various points some readers may hence wish to consult the articles listed at the end of the text. Where possible I have also tried to cite more recent publications, especially from Wales.

The papers in this book were to have appeared in a larger work with the title *Poetry and Devotion in Medieval Britain*, which in 1990 I rashly mentioned in print as forthcoming. This will not now appear. At the time I did not appreciate the reluctance of publishers to accept a first book of this kind. *The Mary of the Celts* is thus a selection (with the advantage of a closely unified theme) from the original plan. But anyone interested in papers from the greater work (on the number of Christ's wounds, the dance of death, the charter of Christ, the cults of St Brigit and St Eligius, Job's gold, Cain's jawbone and *Hamlet*, and the like) will find them easily from my *Medieval Welsh Literature* (Dublin, 1997) or standard bibliographies.

Having lived away from Britain since 1984, I have a special debt to those who have sent me books or offprints over the years, particularly Iestyn Daniel, Marged

Haycock (whose *Blodeugerdd Barddas o Ganu Crefyddol Cynnar* is a major work), Christopher Howse, Nicolas Jacobs, Brian Murdoch, Erich Poppe, Jane Roberts, Salvador Ryan, Nikolai Tolstoy, and Yoko Wada.

This book is a study of literary and artistic motifs in Britain and beyond, which are related to their origins in late antiquity and elsewhere. It is not a devotional or spiritual work. Nevertheless, some will find the testimony of love for the Virgin by Celtic poets and others, extending over many centuries, a moving and impressive record. *Ecce enim ex hoc beatam me dicent omnes generationes*; and so the theme of this book is how that was done in the poetry of medieval Wales and Ireland, as well as their neighbouring countries.

AB

The Annunciation I: Mary, Daughter of her Son

The Annunciation is a convenient place for any study of Marian devotion to begin. It is also a good starting point for Celtic poetry on the Virgin, as it occurs in some of the oldest texts we have, where we find the Virgin praised as the daughter of her own son. Later poetry (discussed below) enlarges upon the paradoxes of the occasion. It declares that the *Ave* 'Hail' of the archangel Gabriel reversed the sorrow brought by *Eva* 'Eve'; or that Mary's virginity remained as pure and intact as a pane of glass through which sunlight shines; or spoke of her simply as vessel of the Holy Trinity. But the theme of Mary as daughter of her son should come first, since it derives from even older sources in the Latin Christianity of North Africa. T. S. Eliot in *Murder in the Cathedral* linked the sanctity of diverse places,

> From where the western seas gnaw at the coast of Iona,
> To the death in the desert, the prayer in forgotten places by the broken imperial column ...

The theme of Mary *mater et filia* 'mother and daughter' also links Africa and Iona (as well as other parts of Britain and Ireland) in unexpected ways.

For the Celtic lands the earliest evidence is not in Welsh or Irish, but Latin. It occurs in a hymn beginning *Cantemus in omni die* 'Let us sing every day', the work of Cú Chuimne of Iona (d. 747), a strange, intricate poem in praise of the Virgin, using a distinctive Hiberno-Latin rhythm and internal rhyme. As such it is a useful reminder of the luxuriant early Latin culture of Ireland and Scotland. Its eighth stanza runs

> Maria, mater miranda,
>   patrem suum edidit,
> Per quem aqua late *lotus*
>   *totus* mundus credidit.[1]

Mary, wondrous mother, bore her own father, through whom the whole world, washed in water, believed.*

How might this theme have reached Cú Chuimne? The answer takes us far from Celtic Scotland. We shall see below that St Augustine's writings would have made the *mater et filia* topos** known in Britain and Ireland at an early date. Yet there is evidence that Cú Chuimne may actually have taken the theme from Spain, from documents of the eleventh Council of Toledo (held in 675) declaring Christ to have been both father and son to the Virgin Mary. At this date Toledo was less remote from Iona than might be thought. The court and schools of Toledo were the home of a brilliant circle of artists and scholars, so it should be thought of as a Spanish Ravenna or Byzantium, the influence of which might well reach the coast of Mull. It can certainly be shown that Cú Chuimne had links with the circle of scholars active at and around Lismore (near Waterford in southern Ireland), which had libraries rich in Spanish texts, including those of the Council of Toledo. The evidence for these links between Toledo, Lismore, and Iona is as follows.

---

* The author's translations here follow each quoted verse.
** topos: 'place'; a rhetorical theme or image.

1. We know the documents of the Council of Toledo were read in Ireland soon after 675, since the Hiberno-Latin scriptural commentary *De Ordine Creaturarum* (written before 700) quotes from them.[2]

2. *De Ordine Creaturarum* also quotes from the daring rationalistic scriptural commentary *De Mirabilibus Sacrae Scripturae*, which was written at Lismore in 655.[3]

3. *De Mirabilibus* and the Toledo documents were therefore studied together in seventh-century Ireland, either at Lismore itself, or a monastery in contact with Lismore.

4. The early eighth-century Irish canon law text *Collectio Canonum Hibernensis* was, according to a ninth-century colophon, compiled by Cú Chuimne of Iona and Ruben of 'Dairinis', the latter identified as a monastery some fourteen miles from Lismore, near Youghal (in County Cork).[4]

5. Despite his links with Iona, then, Cú Chuimne had direct contact with Munster scholars who knew the Toledo documents as they knew other Spanish texts. He was thus well placed to make himself familiar with the canons of the Council of Toledo; and (though a similar expression quoted below was used by St Eusebius) his phrase *Maria, mater miranda, / patrem suum edidit* suggests he actually did so, since clause 48 of the council's documents says of Christ,

Qui tamen secundum quod Deus est, creavit Mariam, secundum quod homo creatus est a Maria: ipse et pater Mariae matris et filius.[5]

The words of Cú Chuimne and the Council of Toledo can be contrasted with expressions for the *mater et filia* topos in St Augustine, such as *a quo invisibili et ipsa creata est ... virgo mater effudit* 'he the unseen who made her, him she bore, mother and maiden', and *creavit Mariam, et creatus est per Mariam* 'he created Mary, and was created by Mary'.[6] These can again be compared with the comments of St Fulgentius of Ruspae (467–532), 'he created the Virgin and was created of the Virgin; and of whom he was the maker, her he made his mother', and St Ildefonsus of Toledo (607–667), 'son of a mother whom he himself had made ... a mother would thus give birth to her maker.'[7]

It is clear these other writers are less direct in their expression of the theme than Cú Chuimne and the Council of Toledo, and that the combination of *mater*, *pater*, and *Maria* apparently occurs only in Cú Chuimne's hymn and the Council's declaration. If the above reasoning is sound, Cú Chuimne's hymn can be recognized, not only as a fine example of the ancient Marian devotion of Ireland and Scotland, but also as reflecting early Spanish devotion to Mary.

Cú Chuimne's debt to the learning of the Church in the other stanzas of this hymn deserves further study, as in its description of Gabriel as bearer of the Word, the contrast of Eve and Mary, its Pauline language of breastplate and helmet, and even its final stanza's image (from the Book of Revelation) of names written in the book of life with angels as witnesses, as if it were a legal document.[8] The topos of *mater et filia* here is of a piece with this vigorous, scriptural imagery.

The Church's learning is also prominent in the oldest known poem in Irish to use the *mater et filia* topos. This much-admired lyric, an anonymous eleventh-century invocation of the Blessed Virgin beginning *A Máire mín, maithingen* 'Gentle Mary, good maiden', applies to the Virgin the prophecies of the Old Testament as interpreted by the medieval Church, the Virgin thus being addressed as 'branch of Jesse's tree', 'choice door through which was born in flesh the shining sun' (cf. Isaiah 11:1 and Ezekiel 44:2). However, the distinctive Irish bardic touch did not desert the poet, so that he calls the 'branch of Jesse's tree' one 'from the fair hazel-grove'. He uses the *mater et filia* topos as follows:

A búadach, a bunata,
  a buidnech, a balc,
guid lem Críst cumachta,
  t'Athair is do Mac.

Thou who art victorious, securely set, retinued, and strong,
pray with me to powerful Christ, who is thy Father and thy
Son.[9]

This stanza is remarkable for two reasons. It addresses the
Virgin, not as an emblem of mildness and obedience found
in many modern countries, both Catholic and Protestant,
but as a figure of power and strength (a tradition nowadays
more familiar in East European countries like Poland or
Russia). The poet is not concerned with exploring the paradoxes of the *mater et filia* topos, unlike some of the writers
below. For him, its importance lies in reinforcing the
Virgin's power. The stanza is also remarkable in containing
what seems to be the oldest example of the *mater et filia*
theme in vernacular poetry. It is characteristic of a poem
that has had much praise.[10] But it is surely predated in
prose by a Christmas homily of Ælfric (*c*.955–*c*.1020), who
closes it by calling Jesus both creator (*scyppend*) and son of
Mary.[11] After the year 1000, then, the topos was being used
in both the English and Irish languages.

A final Irish instance of the *mater et filia* topos comes
from a poem, surviving in a unique copy in Edinburgh,
National Library of Scotland, MS Adv. 72.1.37, the famous
'Book of the Dean of Lismore' written in Perthshire
between 1512 and 1526. The author of the poem, Muireadhach Albanach Ó Dálaigh (*c*.1180–*c*.1250), is famous in
Irish tradition for an incident in 1213 at Lissadell, near
Sligo, where he used an axe to murder a visiting official,
Fionn Ua Brolcháin. Muireadhach then escaped to Scotland, where some of his descendants on South Uist were
still practising as poets in the eighteenth century.[12] Except
for his fifteen years of exile in Scotland (about which he
complained bitterly), Muireadhach took his murder of
Fionn Ua Brolcháin lightly (as did his editor, Bergin). Yet

his devotion to the Virgin and taste for homicide have parallels elsewhere, as with the French professional criminal François Villon, who wrote remarkable poetry to the Virgin Mary, despite murdering a priest.

Muireadhach's poem, beginning *Éistidh riomsa, a Mhuire mhór* 'Listen to me, O great Mary', shows brilliant technical virtuosity. It has been called a work of genius. Even in translation the poem startles by its epithets. When the Virgin and her sisters took husbands, Muireadhach says, 'the three women of the noble heavy-tressed luxuriant hair became slow-footed and pregnant'; while of Mary with child he says, 'your womb was full like the belly of a fish'. He also goes farther than our other writers. God is not only Mary's father and son, but her husband as well; a conceit expressed with unusual tenderness.

> H'Fhear is do Mhac ar do mhuin,
>   geal a ghlac is geal a righ,
> t'Fhearathair réd thaobh as-toigh,
>   ag soin taom d'ealathain t'Fhir.

> There was demonstrated the wisdom of your Husband, that your Husband and your Father was carried by you — bright his hand and bright his arm; your Husband and your Father held close to your side.[13]

By now the image has almost completely entered the ambit of bardic learning, so that Muireadhach's imagery throughout this poem owes far less to the book-learning of the Church that does that of his Irish predecessors. In the stanza quoted here the intellectual paradox of the original *mater et filia* has thus been grafted onto the more tender image of a mother holding a child.

When we turn from Ireland and Scotland to Wales, we find the earliest Welsh example of the theme seems to be that in Aberystwyth, National Library of Wales, MS Llanstephan 27, the 'Red Book of Talgarth' (c.1400). Despite the lateness of the manuscript (named after Talgarth, near Brecon), Sir Ifor Williams described the verses as no later than the twelfth century and perhaps older. Marged Haycock, quoting Jenny Rowland, thinks they might even be as old as the tenth. The sequence begins *Meckyt Meir mab yn y bru* 'Mary fosters a son at her breast', going on to call that son, *Y that, y neirthyat, y brawt*, 'her father, her strengthener, her brother', and continues:

> Ny wyr ny bo kyuarwyd
> Ual y deiryt Meir y gulwyd:
> Y mab, y that, y harglwyd.
>
> Gwnn ual y deiryt Meir, kyt bwyf daerawl — prud,
>   Y'r Drindawt ysprydawl,
> Y mab a'e brawt knawdawl,
> A'e that, arglwyd mat meidrawl.[14]

The untutored do not know how Mary is of kin to God, her son, her father, her lord. I know, though I am but a shame-faced mortal, how Mary is kin to the spiritual Trinity, to her son and her brother in the flesh, and her father, the Lord who blesses and controls.

The lines read like the work of a cleric, and in any case suggest the influence of the Church's learning on Welsh vernacular poetry.

They are paralleled in a passage on the Virgin from a praise poem to God by Gwalchmai ap Meilyr (*fl.* 1130–80), one of a famous dynasty of Gwynedd bards, who has left his mark on the map at the village of Trewalchmai near the A5 in Anglesey. He must be the first British vernacular poet whose home we can still point to.

> Hi yn vam wy thad, hi yn wyry heb wad,
>   Hi yn hollawl rad yn recouyt;
> Hi yn verch wy mab y mot yssyt,
> Hi yn chwaer y Duw o dwywawl fyt.[15]

She is mother to her father, she is a virgin without denial; she is filled with God's grace, generous without stint; she is daughter to her son, it is her privilege; she is sister to God from holy faith.

These lines have attracted the attention of linguists, theologians, and even historians. All praise them. Amongst more recent writers, Rees Davies commented on them as part of a Welsh 'exultation' of Mary, fostered from the twelfth century by the Cistercians and from the thirteenth by the Franciscans; Marged Haycock makes clear the allusion in them to Mary as full of grace, an expression then hotly debated (as noted below) for its implications on the Immaculate Conception, the doctrine that Mary was free from sin from the first moment of her existence; Oliver Davies refers to their 'very sophisticated theological material'.[16] The *mater et filia* topos is also used by Gwalchmai's son, Meilyr (*c*.1170–*c*.1220), in a poem in which he asks for the protection of the angels and saints of heaven against hellfire:

A'm eiryolwy Seint Ezechias
Ar Ueir uam y That, y thec urdas,
A'm eiryolwy Meir ar y Mabkwas
Nat elwyf yn llwgyr yn lloc Idas.[17]

May St Hesychius intercede for me with Mary mother of her father, with her noble magnificence; and may Mary intercede for me with her beloved son, that I do not rot in Judas's den.

'St Hesychius' here seems to be St Hesychius of Jerusalem (d. *c*.450), monk, commentator on the Bible, and homilist, whose sermons show him to be a fervent champion of the dogma of Mary Immaculate. Perhaps that explains his appearance in Welsh poetry. If so, Meilyr's reference to this Greek Father of the Church would be a tribute both to his own learning and to that of the Christian community at Bangor, since (although translations of the Eastern Fathers are commoner in medieval British libraries than might be expected) copies of St Hesychius are very rare. The only surviving copy of his work assigned to a British library of this date is to a twelfth-century one, now Cambridge, Trinity College, MS B.2.9 (= MS 52), from Christ Church, Canterbury.[18] It is possible that the Canterbury manuscript of St Hesychius and Meilyr ap Gwalchmai's reference to him are linked with Canterbury's (often stormy)

involvement in the Diocese of Bangor during this period.
But in any case Bangor possessed contacts with a wider
world of learning; from 1120 to *c.*1139 its bishop was
David the Scot, thought to have been head of the school at
Würzburg, as well as chaplain and chronicler to the Holy
Roman Emperor.[19]

In the next century the theme occurs again, opening a
praise poem to the Virgin by another Anglesey bard,
Gruffudd ap Maredudd (*fl.* 1352–82), who (using a topos
discussed below) also contrasts Mary with Eve:

> Merch mam veir o diweir waet
> chwaer yth dat o rat eiryoet
> eva wyr y aue wyt
> regina anroes eneit.[20]

> Daughter and mother, Mary, sister from sinless blood to your
> Father, from eternal grace a true Eva to *Ave* are you, queen
> who gave us life.

We find the same thought in another poem by Gruffudd:

> Merch a mam a chwaer glaer egluraf
> wyt y grist didrist didranc waessaf.[21]

> Shining and brightest daughter and mother and sister are you
> to Christ, blessed eternal protector.

Gruffudd was part-owner of estates at Aberalaw, Carnedd-
awr, and Dronwy in north-west Anglesey; he was also
household bard to the squires of Penmynydd (near Menai
Bridge), the Welsh ancestors of the Tudor dynasty.
Gruffudd was clearly a man of means who knew something
of the Church's learning, even if he is here content to do no
more than reproduce the phrases of the liturgy.[22]

A variant on the idea of the Virgin as daughter of her
son occurs in a poem beginning *Doeth y'th etholes Iesu*, now
securely attributed to Iolo Goch (*c.*1320–*c.*1400), in which
he declaims praises to the Virgin:

A mam i Dduw yn ymoddiwes,
A merch i'th unbrawd, briffawd broffes,
A chwaer i'th unmab wyd a chares.[23]

And mother to God, comprehending him; and daughter to
your one brother, great destiny's proclamation; and sister to
your one son and his darling are you.

In his poem to the Trinity, the austere puritan Siôn Cent
(*c*.1367–*c*.1430) uses the *mater et filia* topos in words praising God rather than the Blessed Virgin.

Tad y'th gair i Fair Forwyn,
A'i brawd, a'i mab, o bryd mwyn.[24]

Father are you found to the Virgin Mary, and her brother and
son from a fair countenance.

The sequence reverts to praise of the Virgin in a poem to
God by Dafydd Nanmor (*fl*. 1450–80), born in the heart of
Snowdonia, but spending much of his life as a household
bard at Tywyn, between Cardigan and the sea in south-
west Wales.

I Thad a'i Mab doeth ydwyd,
A'i hvn Duw, a'i henaid wyd.
Dy verch a gredaf i oedd,
Duw vy myd, dy vam ydoedd.[25]

Her father and her wise son are you, and her one God and her
life. Your daughter I believe she was and, by heaven, she was
your mother.

But by far the most interesting use of the *mater et filia*
topos in Welsh occurs in two poems, anonymous, but in
the style of Hywel Swrdwal (*fl*. 1430–60), bailiff in 1454–6
of Newtown in Powys, which show signs of ecclesiastical
learning unusual for a Welsh bard. The first is from a
poem to the Virgin beginning *Archwn i Fair a bair byd*:

Dwyn ei mab o'i daioni,
A dwyn ei thad a wnaeth hi.
Bu'r Drindod, is rhod yr haul,
A'i hannedd yn y wennaul.[26]

Out of her goodness she bore her son and her father; the
Trinity dwelt in the bright sun, below the orbit of the sun.

The 'bright sun' here is the Virgin Mary, and the bard is
thinking of Psalm 18:6 (AV 19:4),* translated 'He hath set
his tabernacle in the sun' in the Douay Bible, a verse
applied in exegesis to the moment when, as a work of the
whole Trinity, Christ was conceived in Mary's womb.[27]

The second is from a poem to the Virgin and her parents
beginning *Saint y Cair a Sant Cytus*. The poet's combination of homely images and theological sophistication is
something rare at any date, and marks him out as an original artist. In its economy and 'wit' it is more like medieval
Latin hymnody than much vernacular poetry (especially
poetry in Middle English).

Baich ar ei braich oedd ei brawd
A'i baich a'n dug o bechawd.
Ei thad oedd yn y gadair,
A'i mab oedd yn hyn na Mair.[28]

A burden on her arm was her brother, and her burden
brought us from sin; her father was in the cradle, and her son
was older than Mary was.

In his Marian poem beginning *Y forwyn ofwy arayl*, the
Raglan bard Hywel ap Dafydd ab Ieuan ap Rhys (*fl.*
1450–80) makes his own attempt to respond to the paradoxes of this topos:

ryfeddodd orfod arfoll
yddyn o vyd ddwyn nef oll
dy yn brawd gnawd ganiady
dy dad ath vab da jaith vy

*AV: Authorized Version of the Bible.

merch yth vab wyd lwyd loywdec
amam yth dad mamaeth dec.[29]

A conception that was a triumph and wonder, for a being of
this world to bear the whole of heaven. You allow our brother
flesh, your father and your son, it was a fine thing to say. You
are daughter to your son and mother to your father, fair and
holy one, excellent nurse.

We find the theme used more simply in an anonymous
poem (of the late fifteenth century) from north-west
Wales, in honour of the shrine of Our Lady of the Throne
at Llanystumdwy, near Criccieth:

morwynverch nid mawr anfad
mamaeth yw i mam ai thad
duw n vab diogan a vu
dan vygwyth duw ny vagu.[30]

A daughter and virgin (a great evil it is not), a mother is nurse
to her father [reading *mamaeth yw mam i'w thad*]; God was the
son of the Immaculate, nursing him beneath God's denuncia-
tion.

A final example is cited with the above by Hartwell
Jones from a poem of Lewys Morgannwg (*fl.* 1520–65),
from Llantwit Major in the Vale of Glamorgan.

Mawl mawr vrainiawl Vorwyn
merch vron henferch vrenhinfab
merch honn yw merch i hun mab.

Great praise, O favoured Virgin, the maiden who suckled a
king's son, this maiden is her own son's daughter.

Jones does not give the source of his quotation from
Lewys, but the passage must be early, before Lewys
turned Protestant and abjured his early religious poetry;
as Glanmor Williams points out, in his youth Lewys wrote
two poems to the Marian shrine of Penrhys above the
Rhondda, but may well have rejoiced when the Reformers
came to destroy it.[31]

When we compare instances of the *mater et filia* theme in the Celtic languages with those in English, we find the latter will not detain us long, even if with Chaucer and Donne they include two of the greatest names in English poetry. It is curious that the earliest metrical example of the topos, in a lyric on the Blessed Virgin's joys beginning *Seinte marie leuedi brist*, is as late as the thirteenth century. The only known copy of this lyric is in Cambridge, Trinity College, MS B.14.39 (= 323), a manuscript compiled about 1255–60, perhaps by Franciscans, in the Worcester/ Hereford area.

> Seinte marie, moder milde,
> Thi fader bi-com to one childe.[32]

A more developed example occurs in the opening lines of a poem by William Herebert (d. 1333), a Hereford Franciscan.

> Thou wommon boute fere
> Thine owne fader bere;
> Gret wonder this was,
> That on wommon was moder
> To fader and hire brother,
> So never other nas.[33]

Rosemary Woolf pointed out how this 'witty' exploration of the paradoxes of the topos is something rare in Middle English verse, in contrast to much Latin and French poetry and, we might add, some of the Welsh instances quoted above. The topos occurs again in Herebert's translation of *Alma redemptoris mater*:

> In the thou bere thyn holy uader,
> That mayden were after and rather.[34]

In Geoffrey Chaucer (d. 1400) the theme appears in *The Second Nun's Prologue* from *The Canterbury Tales*, where the nun addresses the Blessed Virgin,

Thow Mayde and Mooder, doghter of thy Sone,
Thow welle of mercy, synful soules cure,
In whom that God for bountee chees to wone.[35]

These lines are also a translation into English, in this case
from the opening lines of canto xxxiii of Dante's *Paradiso*
quoted below. The theme also appears, briskly, in a brief
fifteenth-century Scottish hymn to the Virgin in a
sixteenth-century manuscript (illustrated with woodcuts
from printed books) perhaps intended for use in a Scottish
religious house:

Haill! quene of hevin, and steren of blis;
Sen that thi sone thi fader is,
How suld he ony thing the warn [refuse],
And thou his mother, and he thi barne?[36]

But it is in the poetry of John Donne (1572–1631) that the
finest instance of this idea occurs. Donne's poetry is rich in
medieval ideas used with a force rare in medieval English,
nowhere in more concentrated form than in the poem
'Annunciation' from his *Holy Sonnets*, where Donne
addresses the Virgin:

Ere by the spheares time was created, thou
Wast in his minde, who is thy Sonne, and Brother,
Whom thou conceiv'st, conceiv'd; yea thou art now
Thy Makers maker, and thy Fathers mother … [37]

As regards the rest of Europe and examples in Continental vernaculars, we may note some of the early
instances quoted by Mayer. These include examples in
German from a Marian poem (perhaps of the twelfth
century) written in the lower Rhineland, the apocrypha of
Walther von der Vogelweide (d. *c.*1230), and the *Goldene
Schmiede* of Konrad von Würzburg (d. 1287); in French
from Wace (d. *c.*1175); in Italian from Dante; and in
Galician-Portuguese from a lyric by Alfonso X of Castile
(1221–1284).[38]
Some of the examples cited by Mayer, together with a

few from other sources, will suggest the qualities of those in Irish, Welsh, and English above. Wace's poem on the Virgin's Assumption uses the topos with an elegant simplicity, as one might expect, with Christ saying to his mother,

> Bele très douce chere mere
> Quant je qui estoie ton pere.

Of unusual sophistication are lines, by a poet clearly delighting in paradox, in a thirteenth-century Continental French lyric quoted by Rosemary Woolf:

> Li fruiz planta l'arbre dont il issi
> Et dou ruissel descendi la fontainne,
> L'uevre l'ouvrier aleva et norri
> Et li solaus vint de la tresmontainne.[39]

In contrast, Anglo-Norman verse rarely rises above a 'mediocre ease'.

> Douce dame, pie mere
> de ky nasqui vostre pere.[40]

Provençal verse presents the classic rhetorical patterns in, for example, the poem *Ajssi quon es sobronrada* by Guiraut Riquier (*c.*1230–after 1292) of Narbonne, where the poet asks for the intercession of the Virgin Mary, whose face looks forever on God:

> ... lo rey glorios
> qu'es paires e filhs de vos,
> filla del vostre filh, maire
> del vostre paire: com faire
> so's poc es grans meravilla.[41]

The glorious king who is your father and your son, O daughter of your son, mother of your father: a great wonder it is how this could be.

The same pattern is repeated in another poem by Alfonso X of Castile (d. 1284), in his *Cantiga* on the Assumption:

Beêita es Maria, Filla, Madre e criada
de Deus, teu Padre e teu Fillo.[42]

Blessed is Mary, daughter, mother, and handmaid of God, your father and your son.

In the earlier fourteenth century, Juan Ruiz, archpriest of Hita and author of *Libro de buen amor*, treats the theme somewhat minimally when naming the first of the seven joys of the Virgin.

El primero
fue, certero,
ángel a ti mensajero
del Espíritu Santo:
Conçebiste a tu Padre.[43]

The first, certainly, was the angel messenger to you from the Holy Spirit: you conceived your Father.

Yet poets in the various languages of Spain, including Catalan, seem to have made little of the tremendous paradoxes of the *mater et filia* topos. It would have been a good theme for the rhetorical Catherine wheels and Roman candles of Calderón's plays (as shown below in his use of the sunbeam-through-glass topos). On this, Welsh and Irish poets quoted above can hold their own against other poets from the rest of Europe.

So the wide diffusion of the theme is very clear. But how did it originate? It is well known that it is one of the oldest paradoxes applied to Mary, and that it received wide circulation from the sermons and scriptural commentaries of St Augustine of Hippo (354–430), who used it repeatedly. Its popularity increased further with its use in the sixth-century hymn *Quem terra, pontus, aethera* and the eleventh-century antiphon *Alma redemptoris mater*, both of which were added to the liturgy. The topos thus became common in medieval and later European literature, most famously in the line *Vergine Madre, Figlia del tuo Figlio* that opens canto xxxiii of Dante's *Paradiso*.

Yet it is surprising to find how much the theme was developed and elaborated by the medieval writers quoted above from its relatively sober use in late Antiquity. In his fundamental study (though it hardly mentions Insular sources), Anton Mayer of Freising, near Munich, emphasized its scriptural parallels, but also its roots in the highly stylized rhetorical and even grammatical structures of literary Greek and Latin, with their love of studied antithesis. Writing in the belief that the idea occurs first in St Augustine, Mayer linked it with the *sponsus et filius* topos appearing, for example, in the *Tractatus* of St Zeno (d. *c*.371), a North African who became Bishop of Verona. St Zeno's phrase is,

Mira res, concipit Maria de ipso quem parit ... capitque virgo, quem mundus mundique non capit plenitudo.[44]

A great wonder, Mary conceives of him whom she bears ... and a virgin receives him, whom the world and its fullness rejects.

Mayer argued that this topos reappears, brilliantly modified, in Augustine's paradox of *mater et filia*: for example, in Augustine's description in his sermon 189 of Christ as *creatus est de ea, quam creavit*, and in his scriptural commentaries.

Yet recent scholarship modifies Mayer's conclusions by adding to the instances collected by him, and showing that the concept of *mater et filia* actually predates Augustine. A striking instance of this occurs in *De Trinitate Confessio*, somewhat shakily attributed to St Eusebius of Vercelli (d. 371), which says of Christ:

Quod tamen secundum quod est Deus creavit Mariam, secundum quod homo est creatus ex Maria, ipse Pater Mariae matris suae, et Filius.[45]

In that he is God, he made Mary; in that he is man, he was made by Mary: he is the father of Mary his mother, and her son.

Another example occurs in *Hymni de Beata Maria*, written in Syriac and attributed to St Ephraem of Syria (*c*.306–373). In these oriental hymns, remarkable for their extravagant praise of the Virgin and their tender meditation on the love between her and her child, the Blessed Virgin is represented as declaring,

> Fili mi, quem peperi, senior me es; Domine mi, quem portavi, sustines me.[46]

> My son, to whom I gave birth, you are older than I; my Lord, whom I carried in my arms, you hold me up.

Though there have been doubts (which their use of the *mater et filia* topos may reinforce) on the authenticity of both the above texts, the *Hymni* cannot postdate the fifth or sixth century; and in any case the authenticity of the following Greek text, *De Trinitate* by Didymus of Alexandria (313–*c*.398), is certain. In his discussion of the words describing Jesus as the Virgin's firstborn in Matthew 1:25, *peperit filium suum primogenitum*, Didymus says of Christ,

> eius primogenitus recte vocatus est qui et ipsam, et omnes formavit.[47]

> Rightly was he called her first-born who shaped her and all things.

So it is Didymus who has the honour of being the first writer known to have used this paradox, as part of the Greek culture of fourth-century Alexandria.

The use of the topos by two writers in the West, active on what is now French soil, is also worth noting. In his polemical *De Incarnatione Christi* of 429–30, John Cassian (*c*.360–*c*.432) of Lérins says,

Vides ergo quod non solum, inquam, antiquiorem se Maria peperit: non solum, inquam, antiquiorem se, sed auctorem sui, et procreans procreatorem suum, facta est parentis parens ... [48]

So you see, then, that Mary not only gave birth to one older than herself: not only, then, older than herself, but the maker of herself, and she became her parent's parent, bringing forth her creator ...

St Venantius Fortunatus (*c*.530–*c*.600) of Poitiers turns the same idea into elegiacs:

Unde tuum, mater, generas natum atque parentem:
  Hinc prolem, inde patrem: hoc Deus, illud humus.[49]

And so, O mother, you beget a son and father: a child here, a parent there: God is this, clay is that.

However, the stanza in the hymn to the Virgin Mary, *Quem terra, pontus, aethera*, probably by a disciple of Venantius, was even more influential.

O gloriosa femina,
excelsa super sidera,
qui te creavit provide
lactas sacrato ubere.[50]

This was turned into English by a fourteenth-century cleric (perhaps a preacher called Oliver):

Lefdy blisful, of muchel miht,
Heyere thanne the sterres liht,
Hym the the made wumman best
Thou youe hym souken of thi brest.[51]

With the examples above can be placed those quoted by Mayer from Caelius Sedulius (*fl. c*.450), St Peter Chrysologus (d. *c*.450) of Imola, near Bologna, Hrotsvith (*fl. c*.950) of Gandesheim, near Hannover, St Peter Damian (d. 1072),

Adam of St Victor (*fl. c.*1140), St Elizabeth of Schönau (1129–65), Walter of Châtillon (d. 1184), Ulrich Stöcklin (d. 1443) of Wessobrunn, near Munich, and Thomas à Kempis (d. 1471). Of the many instances quoted by Mayer from anonymous Latin hymns, one in particular is too famous to leave out: the phrase *tu quae genuisti / natura mirante tuum sanctum genitorum* 'you who, to the astonishment of nature, gave birth to your own holy creator' from *Alma redemptoris mater*, an antiphon (perhaps German and eleventh-century) formerly attributed to Hermann the Lame (d. 1054) of Reichenau, by Lake Constance.[52]

But it is a matter for reflection whether the most successful treatment of this theme, Dante's excepted, is in poetry at all. It is perhaps in sculpture, in Michelangelo's *Pietà* at St Peter's in Rome, that we see art most nearly approximating to the nobility and tenderness of this enigmatic theme. There we see a Madonna whose features have been sculpted to show a maturity which is nevertheless unmarked by time, whose form is that of a young woman, but who is yet supernaturally great, 'like the antique Demeter'; and who holds the body of a Christ older than herself, but who yet shows in her countenance 'the quiet expression of a strong woman in her full and unspoiled beauty'.[53]

If the *mater et filia* topos allowed writers for a thousand years and more to dwell upon the mysteries of the Incarnation, the contrast of Eva and Mary gave them further scope. A common feature of medieval texts is thus wordplay on the *Ave* of Gabriel's greeting to the Virgin Mary, and the name Eva. Eva brought sorrow to mankind, but *Ave* at the Annuciation brought joy. This palindrome, variously developed throughout Europe, received special attention in Wales, where *Ave* became a somewhat unexpected part of a rationale for poetry.

The contrast of Eve and Mary, dating from St Justin Martyr and St Irenaeus of Lyon in the second century, is standard in the Fathers.[54] But the first text actually known to play on *Ave* and *Eva* is the anonymous hymn *Ave maris stella*, dated to the ninth century.

Sumens illud Ave
Gabrielis ore,
Funda nos in pace,
Mutans nomen Evae.[55]

Receiving that 'Ave' from the lips of Gabriel, establish us in peace, changing Eva's name.

Ave maris stella was known early in England: it appears in London, British Library, MS Add. 37517, the 'Bosworth Psalter' written in the late tenth century, probably at Christ Church, Canterbury, or perhaps Westminster Abbey. The hymn figured later in the Sarum Rite and Little Hours of the Virgin, becoming familiar to millions of medieval Christians. It first occurs in a manuscript of the ninth century from Sankt Gallen, Switzerland, and may be no older than that.[56] Of the verse quoted above there are many Latin imitations.[57]

When we turn from Latin texts with the *Ave*-Eva word-play to English ones, we find the oldest verse instance in the thirteenth-century song *Of on that is so fayr and bright*, where a Latin context remains strong:

Al this world was forlore
    Eva peccatrice
Tyl our lord was ybore
    De te genetrice;
With *Ave* it went away,
Thuster nyth, and com the day
    Salutis.[58]

The poem, in North Midland or Northern dialect, is found in a thirteenth-century hand in London, British Library, MS Egerton 613, and in Cambridge, Trinity College, MS B.14.39 (= 323), the latter being a collection of preaching material mentioned above, which was compiled (probably by friars) in the Worcester-Hereford area *c*.1255–60.

A determined effort to bring the topos fully into English occurs in *Heyl, leuedy, se stoerre bryht*, a translation of *Ave maris stella*:

Thylk 'aue' that thou vonge in spel
Of the aungeles mouth kald Gabriel
In gryht [security] ous sette and shyld vrom shome
That turnst abakward Eues nome.[59]

This is a further poem by William Herebert (d. 1333), a Franciscan of Hereford. His translation can be compared with another in a preaching-book (now Oxford, Merton College, MS 248) of Bishop Sheppey of Rochester (d. 1360):

taket an that ilke gretyn vncowthe
that the was sayd of Gabriel mowthe,
settand man in pes ful fane,
tornand the name of heue a-gayne.[60]

A later fourteenth-century instance occurs in an ambitious acrostic poem on the *Ave Maria* in Cambridge, University Library, MS Gg.4.32 (probably once in the possession of a cleric), where the implications of the topos are drawn out:

Wymmen weren alle ischente,
In thraldom helde and onworthlie,
Thorgh eue that the deuel blente,
What iesu crist with his maistrie
Tho lettres of hire name wente,
And made of eua aue marie,
And clansing sente
To wymmen of ech vileinie.[61]

At the other extreme, the refrain of a fifteenth-century carol puts the idea into a nutshell:

Nova, nova:
'Aue' fit ex 'Eua'.[62]

A variant version of the theme appears in fifteenth-century English drama, in the N-town cycle (in East Anglian dialect), where Gabriel, etymologizing *Ave* as 'A vae', greets the Virgin with the words:

Heyl fful of grace, God is with the,
Amonge all women blyssyd art thu.
Here this name Eva is turnyd Aue:
That is to say withowte sorwe ar ye now.[63]

An even more elaborate working-out of the theme occurs in *The Myroure of Oure Ladye,* an anonymous devotional tract written in the earlier fifteenth century for the Bridgettine nuns of Syon, near Isleworth, Middlesex.[64] Finally, the ghost of the *Ave*-Eva locution lurks in *Paradise Lost,* V.385–7, in reference to Eve:

on whom the angel 'Hail'
Bestowed, the holy salutation used
Long after to blest Mary, second Eve.[65]

When we turn from English to Continental languages, we find that whereas English often uses the topos clumsily, French elaborates it with finesse. An early example is provided by Gautier de Coinci (1177–1236), a monk at Saint-Médard de Soissons, who later became prior of Vic-sur-Aisne.[66] By the time we reach Huon le Roi of Cambrai (*c.*1250), in his *Li 'Ave Maria' en Roumans,* the theme is being used with *élan*:

Pour EVA fu li mons plains d'ire,
Mais AVE joie nous raporte:
Pour AVE ovri Dius la porte
De paradis, qui fourbatue
Fu lonc tans, par coi fu batue
Mainte ame par devens [= 'in'] enfer.[67]

With this we can compare lines in *Dame des Cius* by Guillaume le Vinier (d. 1245), one of a circle of writers at Arras in Artois, which read *Ave* as *a vae* 'from woe':

Mout nous troubla
Cele que Diex forma,
Nom ot Eva,
Par li estiens dampné.

Par la bonté
La Virgene od saintée
   Diex ot pité,
La lettre retorna
   Avant mist *A*,
Et au daerrain *ve*,
Pour *Eva* dist *Ave*,
Par quoi somes sauvé.[68]

Watriquet de Couvin, a Liègeois writing near Namur in
the early fourteenth century, used the theme with sophisticated rhyming:

Eve nous empetra l'avé
qui le pechié d'Adam lava
et nous geta d'enfer la bas
qui n'en est purgiez ne lavez.[69]

In Provençal, Lanfranc Cigala (d. 1257 or 1258), a
Genoese who was an unlikely combination of magistrate,
ambassador, merchant, and poet, contrasted Eve (who
assented to the word of Satan) with the Virgin Mary (who
assented to the word of God):

Eva ac nom l'enemia;
   el contradig
   segon l'escrig
ditz hom: 'Ave' Maria.
Tot so qu'Eva desvia,
   Maire de Dieu,
'ave' torn' en la via.[70]

In Spain the motif appears in Portuguese-Galician dialect
in the above-mentioned *Cantigas de Santa María* of Alfonso
X. Between *Ave* and *Eva* there is great contrast, because
Eva deprived us of Paradise and God, but *Ave* gave them
back:

Entre Av'e Eva,
gran departiment'á.

Ca Eva nos tolleu
o Parays', e Deus
Ave nos y meteu;
porend', amigos meus,
   Entre Av'e Eva.[71]

The theme even occurs in twentieth-century Catalan poetry, in J. M. López-Picó's sonnet *El Seny de Mon*, where the ancient word of the angelic greeting renews Eve's hopes:

Del mot antic l'adverament angèlic
rejoveneix les esperances d'Eva.[72]

When we move from Spain to Wales, we find the first Welsh bard to use the topos was Gruffudd ap Maredudd (*fl.* 1352–82).[73] We have met him before, as an Anglesey landowner who wrote praise-poems to the ancestors of the Tudor dynasty, as well as a fine poem to the Chester Rood.[74] He uses the *Ave*-Eva topos in the opening lines of a Marian poem already quoted:

Merch mam veir o diweir waet
chwaer yth dat o rat eiryoet
eva wyr y aue wyt
regina anroes eneit.[75]

Daughter and mother, Mary, sister from sinless blood to your Father, from eternal grace a true Eva to *Ave* are you, queen who gave us life.

More remarkable is Gruffudd's use of the theme for a complete poem:

Teir llythyren wenn windut
   an duc ynghyvyrgoll gollet
   a their veir o vawr garyat
   an duc nef on dygyn ovit
teir veir oleugreir a vawrlygrawd — byt
   o lythyr bryt wyt wahawd
A their o nef uthur y nawd
   oe gwiw rat an gwaredawd

E.v.a. bu pla ym pob plas
yn bwrw y berigyl gyweithyas
A.v.e. urdedic urdas
an duc yn veith o geith gas
Goleu vyd veir vam geli
golwc ratlawn heb gelu
gofwy nef oed dec ave
goual vu aual eua
Da y gwnaeth ryd o gaeth drwy goeth gannwyll
wyry wirion heul y doeth bwyll
o ual amyl aual amhwyll
aue dec rac eua dwyll.[76]

Three fair letters in paradise brought us total loss in perdi-
tion; and three, Mary, out of great love brought us heaven
from our sore affliction. Three, Mary, light's holy treasure,
that made great spoil of the world, through a letter that
invited the mind to sin; and three from heaven of awesome
protection out of its excellent grace saved us. E.v.a. was
plague in every place, casting mankind into peril; a.v.e., noble
honour, brought us at length from a hateful bond. A light is
Mary, mother of the Lord, a sight full of grace without
concealment; a visitation from heaven was fair *ave*, but
sorrow was Eva's apple. Well did the sun of her pure discre-
tion make bondmen free, through the fair candle of a pure
virgin, from the great tax of folly's apple; a fair *Ave* against
deceitful Eva.

The theme is used by another Anglesey poet and household bard to the Tudurs of Penmynydd, Gruffudd Fychan
ap Gruffudd ab Ednyfed Fychan. It now seems accepted
that Gruffudd Fychan wrote *c.*1370–90 rather than
*c.*1320.[77] He uses the topos in a metrical expansion of the
Ave Maria beginning *Anrec wladeid nys treid traet*, which
tells how man, despite condemnation by Eve's folly, was
redeemed through the Annunciation. The *Ave*-Eva topos
occurs in the lines,

Aue rac mawrdrwc aual
Maria eua ovul

Geireu gobrwyeu gabriel
Gracia lles awna yn ol.[78]

Ave, against the great misfortune, *Maria*, of foolish Eve's
apple, Words, the gifts of Gabriel, *Gracia*, benefited us after.

But the most remarkable use of the motif comes in a poem
by Rhys Goch Eryri (fl. *c*.1385–*c*.1448), a native of Snowdonia who was buried at Beddgelert. In *c*.1425–30 Rhys
engaged in mild literary skirmishing with Llywelyn ap
Moel y Pantri (d. 1440) of Llanwnnog, north of Caersws in
Powys.[79] In one poem from the controversy (which has the
air of a Christmas game), Rhys defends *awen* (poetic gift,
genius, or inspiration, 'muse') by identifying the first three
letters of the Welsh word with the *Ave* of Gabriel's salua-
tion, and the last letter the *n* of *nef* 'heaven'. For Rhys, the
muse thus had the same nature as the Holy Spirit, and the
inspiration of the bards in praising the great ones of the
world therefore came from heaven (and not, as the bard
Siôn Cent had discordantly riposted, from hell).[80] In a
poem beginning *Dewrddrud Lywelyn daerddraig*, Rhys says
in reply to Llywelyn:

Pond *a* ac *u*, gu gywir,
O gun wawd, ac *e* yn wir
A roes Duw, o'i ras y dêl,
Er gobr yng ngenau Gabriel?
A Gabriel yn air gobraff,
Da gwn gred, a'i dug yn graff
O'r nef gatholig ar naid,
Fawr gynnydd, ar Fair gannaid.
Ysbryd, Tad urddad eurddellt,
Glân, a Mab goleuni mellt,
O'r tair llythyren, air teg,
Byw fireinryw fu'r anrheg.
Drwy unrhyw lythr, dro iawnrodd,
A'n balch gelfyddyd o'n bodd,
Yr ysgrifennir, wir wen,
Da pyrth Duw, deuparth d'awen;
A rhan o henw, Fenw faenol,
A nef gyda hynny'n ôl,

Gwrdd ennill, gerddau anian;
Ac am hyn, Lywelyn lân,
Doedaist, y diau wawdydd,
Yn eglur, ffyrf fesur ffydd,
Mur uchder mydr mawr, echdoe,
Ym iawn ddysg am awen ddoe,
Enaid y beirdd, onid bod,
Gorau Beibl, gair heb wybod.
Gwrdd yr atebaist deg iach
A huawdl ymy haeach,
Daith ddifagl y doeth Efa
O nef ddoe am na fai dda.
Felly doeth awen gennym,
Gwrdd ras, yn fam y gerdd rym.[81]

My friend, are not *a* and *u* and *e* in truth fine poetry, that God gave (may it come from his grace) for recompense in the mouth of Gabriel? And well do I know the doctrine that in an instant Gabriel, as the mighty Word, brought it, great blessing, steadfastly from faithful heaven in a moment to radiant Mary. The Father, exalted, gold-rodded, the Son, light of thunderbolts, and Holy Spirit: from the three letters of fair greeting the gift was beautiful and alive. Through the same letters at the moment of a just gift and our proud art with our assent, there is written down fit and true (well does God give help) the two portions of your *awen*, and a share of the name, O landed Menw, with heaven after that, mighty gains, songs of nature. And on this, my dear Llywelyn, you said the day before yesterday as a true poet and clearly, as a sure measure of faith and high bulwark of great verse, fitting teaching concerning the *awen* yesterday, that the soul of poets, until it is a word without knowledge, is the best Bible. You have answered me fairly, well, eloquently, and almost completely. A perfect message came from heaven yesterday because Eve sinned; and so the *awen* came to us, a fine grace, as mother of mighty song.

Although the theory of poetry set out here is well known to Celticists, it deserves attention from others as a unique defence of poetic inspiration.[82]

The *Ave*-Eva topos remained popular in fifteenth-century Wales, as is shown by *Archwn i Fair a bair byd*, an

anonymous Marian poem (already quoted) from the
school of Hywel Swrdwal of Newtown, Powys.

> Gabriel, drwy loywdeg wybren,
> Anfones i santes wen
> Afe, am bechod Efa;
> A Mair a'i dug, mawr ei da.[83]

> Gabriel, through bright heavens, addressed to this holy saint
> *Ave*, for sinful Eva; Mary bore that, great her grace.[84]

Association of *Ave* with the Virgin was so familiar to the
bards that Guto'r Glyn (fl. *c.*1440–*c.*1493), in a poem of
after *c.*1480 thanking Dean Richard Kyffin of Bangor for a
rosary, alludes to the word as her 'three letters':

> Mae Mair, a'i thair llythyren,
> Mae'r Mab Rhad mawr ymhob pren.[85]

> There is Mary and her three letters, there is the great Son of
> Grace in every bead.

It is curious that 'three letters' for Gabriel's *Ave* is paralleled in Middle High German, and survives in a modern
German proverb, 'Drei Buchstaben machen uns eigen und
frei.'[86]

Expert use of the topos is made by Dafydd ab Edmwnd
(*fl.* 1450–90), poet and gentleman of Hanmer, Flintshire, in
the opening lines of a Marian poem.

> Mair em ddiwair mam dduw ion
> mawr enw wyd ir morynion
> yth ovyn i dauth avi
> yn gennad duw tad i ti
> Eva an dyg i ovyn
> avi o honod ti an tynn
> di ryvedd wedyr avi
> duw vab duw yw dy vab di[87]

> Mary, immaculate gem, mother of the Lord God, a great
> name are you amongst virgins. To ask you there came *Ave* as

a message from God the Father to you. *Eva* led us into fear; but your *Ave* rescues us. Small wonder that, after *Ave*, God the Son of God is your son.

The above survey allows certain conconclusions. First, it indicates how widespread *Ave*-Eva wordplay was in medieval poetry. The above list of examples can no doubt be added to. Second, it reveals misunderstandings in standard works. It has been claimed that the wordplay is 'found in the writings of many Latin Fathers' and that its later medieval popularity 'probably arose through its occurrence in the Latin writings of St Bernard of Clairvaux'.[88] Yet both statements seem unfounded. The topos is not patristic; and its popularity is due to *Ave maris stella*, as the translations indicate.

Finally, the material above modifies one editor's condemnation of such Latin clichés, 'subject to slight variations in wording which in no way lift them out of the class of pious commonplace', occurring in medieval English carols. Declaring it would be 'as useless as it would be dull to reproduce here the catalogue of these Latin expressions', described as 'uninspired' and showing 'lack of distinction', he cites *Ave fit ex Eva* as the first of them.[89]

But the use of the expression by Gruffudd ap Maredudd and Rhys Goch Eryri shows that what in English is dull, is in Welsh the opposite. Rhys Goch Eryri uses the topos in debate for a crucial purpose: to justify his role as a professional poet. His use of the *Ave*-Eva topos thus does more than show medieval Latin influence on the vernacular. It shows the bards able to extract powerful arguments from unpromising material, producing a nimble, serious verse debate on poetry and the role of the poet, which would be famous if it had not been written in a minority language such as Welsh.

Notes

1. Dreves and Blume, ii. p. 266; O'Dwyer, *Mary*, p. 55; Clancy and Márkus, *Iona*, p. 184.
2. Madoz, *Symbole*, pp. 33, 79, 99; Díaz, pp. 26–7, 36, 86–7; Lapidge and Sharpe, *Bibliography*, p. 98; McNamara, 'Celtic Christianity', pp. 6–7.
3. Chadwick, *Age of the Saints*, pp. 112–13; Díaz, p. 37; Bischoff, 'Turning-Points', p. 144; Lapidge and Sharpe, *Bibliography*, p. 79.
4. Kenney, *Sources*, pp. 248–9; Hughes, *Church*, pp. 123, 132–3; O'Dwyer, *Célí Dé*, p. 37.
5. Madoz, *Symbole*, p. 90.
6. Mayer, 'Mater et filia', p. 67; Madoz, *Symbole*, p. 90.
7. Mayer, 'Mater et filia', p. 73; Madoz, *Symbole*, p. 91.
8. O'Dwyer, *Mary*, pp. 54–6; cf. also Herbert, *Iona*.
9. Murphy, pp. 48, 49.
10. Ó Laoghaire, 'Mary', p. 50; O'Dwyer, 'An Mhaighdean Mhuire', p. 71, and his *Mary*, p. 67.
11. Godden, p. 11.
12. Flower, pp. 85–8.
13. Bergin, pp. 97, 256; O'Dwyer, *Mary*, p. 91.
14. Haycock, pp. 117, 118; Breeze, *Medieval Welsh Literature*, pp. 56–8.
15. Henry Lewis, p. 24.
16. Caerwyn Williams, 'Beirdd y Tywysogion', pp. 87–8, and his *Canu Crefyddol*, pp. 26–7; Myrddin Lloyd, pp. 24–5; Simon Evans, *Writers*, p. 16; R. R. Davies, *Wales 1063–1415*, p. 207; Haycock, p. 116; Oliver Davies, *Celtic Christianity*, pp. 101–2.
17. Henry Lewis, p. 64; Breeze, *Medieval Welsh Literature*, p. 38.
18. N. R. Ker, p. 31.
19. Glanmor Williams, pp. 2–4, 6, 23–4.
20. Owen Jones, p. 312; Gwenogvryn Evans, col. 1200.
21. Gwenogvryn Evans, col. 1213.
22. *Dictionary of Welsh Biography*, pp. 312–13.
23. Johnston, *Gwaith Iolo Goch*, p. 139.
24. Ifor Williams and Thomas Roberts, p. 296.
25. Thomas Roberts of Wrexham, p. 92.
26. Ifor Williams and Thomas Roberts, p. 93; cf. Clancy, *Medieval Welsh Lyrics*, p. 162.
27. Cf. Gray, *Selection*, pp. 101–2.
28. Ifor Williams and Thomas Roberts, p. 96.
29 E. Stanton Roberts, p. 158.
30. Hartwell Jones, p. 337; cf. Glanmor Williams, p. 491.
31. Hartwell Jones, p. 337 n. 7; Glanmor Williams, pp. 490–1.
32. Brown, *English Lyrics of the XIIIth Century*, p. 28; cf. Woolf,

English Religious Lyric, p. 132.
33. R. T. Davies, p. 95; cf. Woolf, *English Religious Lyric*, pp. 132–3, and Gray, p. 90.
34. Brown, *Religious Lyrics of the XIVth Century*, p. 22.
35. Benson, p. 262.
36. Gray, *Selection*, pp. 69, 121.
37. Cf. Woolf, *English Religious Lyric*, p. 133; Gray, *Themes*, p. 91.
38. Mayer, pp. 76–9.
39. Woolf, *English Religious Lyric*, p. 132.
40. Ibid.
41. Oroz p. 212, and cf. pp. 326–7.
42. Herrán, p. 369.
43. Ibid., p. 353.
44. Mayer, p. 72; cf. Casagrande, p. 285.
45. Casagrande, p. 169.
46. Casagrande, p. 262; cf. Woolf, *English Religious Lyric*, p. 116.
47. Casagrande, p. 388.
48. Ibid., p. 679.
49. Ibid., p. 1236.
50. Raby, p. 92; Woolf, *English Religious Lyric*, p. 131.
51. Brown, *Religious Lyrics of the XIVth Century*, p. 53.
52. Raby, p. 226; Woolf, *English Religious Lyric*, p. 131.
53. Hirn, p. 281.
54. Woolf, *English Religious Lyric*, pp. 115–16.
55. Raby, p. 226.
56. Ker, *Catalogue*, pp. 161–2; Korhammer, pp. 173–87; Gneuss, p. 420; Remiger, i. p. 317.
57. Salzer, pp. 476–87; Raby, p. 368.
58. Gray, pp. 83–4, 86; cf. Greene, p. 126.
59. Silverstein, p. 44; Gray, p. 83.
60. Brown, *Religious Lyrics of the XIVth Century*, p. 55.
61. Ibid., p. 233.
62. Greene, p. 151.
63. Gray, p. 84; cf. Spector.
64. Bridgett, p. 49.
65. Gray, p. 83.
66. Becker, p. 51; Hirn, p. 373.
67. Huon le Roi, i. p. 17.
68. Chambers and Sidgwick, p. 347, and cf. p. 350.
69. Alfonso X, p. 111.
70. Oroz, p. 314.
71. Herrán, p. 103.
72. Ibid., p. 478.
73. Myrddin Lloyd, p. 22.

74. *Dictionary of Welsh Biography*, pp. 312–13.
75. Gwenogvryn Evans, col. 1200 (with 'vair' supplied in line one).
76. Gwenogvryn Evans, col. 1329, with readings from Lloyd-Jones, pp. 97, 681.
77. Lloyd-Jones, pp. 289, 571, 593; D. R. Johnston, p. 8.
78. Gwenogvryn Evans, col. 1294.
79. Ruddock, pp. 183–4.
80. Glanmor Williams, p. 237.
81. Ifor Williams and Thomas Roberts, p. 171; on Menw, Arthur's magician, see Bromwich and Evans, pp. 75–6.
82. Ifor Williams, 'Cywydd', pp. 47–8; Brynley Roberts, p. 78.
83. Ifor Williams and Thomas Roberts, p. 93; cf. Glanmor Williams, p. 482.
84. Clancy, *Medieval Welsh Lyrics*, p. 162.
85. J. Ll. Williams and Ifor Williams p. 249.
86. Ifor Williams, 'Ave, Eva', p. 334; cf. E. I. Rowlands pp. 345, 533.
87. Thomas Roberts of Bangor, p. 117.
88. Blake, p. 106.
89. Greene, p. lxxxv; Welsh instances outdo even those in Gray, *Selection*, p. 84.

The Annunciation II: God's Sunbeam and the Holy Trinity

The hope of Christ's incarnation became immediate when Gabriel greeted Mary with *Ave*: its wonder was shown by the *mater et filia* topos. Two other themes elaborated the paradoxes of the event. A sunbeam through glass symbolized Mary's unstained purity; and the role there of the Trinity was shown by images of Mary with all three Persons I think in her womb.

First, the sunbeam through glass. As with the *mater et filia* motif, this is a product of the classical world, specifically of the late Latin culture of North Africa. It expresses the idea that, as light shines through glass, but the glass remains perfect and undamaged, so Mary's virginity remained perfect and entire after she had conceived and given birth to her son. What follows brings together examples of this in Celtic and then other languages, discusses its use in art, and describes its Christian Latin origins.[1]

In the Celtic languages the motif appears earliest in Irish, where four bards have been thought to refer to it, and where it has been derived (without reason) from St Ambrose (d. 397).

i. Donnchadh Mór Ó Dálaigh (d. 1244), in a poem on Christ's Passion:

> A Sbiorad Dé fa docht rún
> ní hé do chorp an corp criadh
> corp Moire rod léig n-a lár
> mar théid tré chlár ngloine an ghrian.

O Spirit of God, steadfast of will, not thine was the body which Mary received within her, as the sun passes through glass.[2]

ii. Muircheartach Ó Cionga (*c.1580?*), in a poem on Christ and the Virgin:

Coinne rúin is rífhriotail,
lúth toile 'n-a thréineitibh
le cóir ngráidh mar ghréineatail
do-chóidh san óigh d'éineitil.

Borne on a wind of love and having the eagerness of desire in his strong wings, the Lord with one swoop entered as a sunbeam into the Virgin's womb; 'twas a meeting of love and princely converse.[3]

iii. Aonghus ó Dálaigh (*c.1600*), working perhaps in west Munster:

Táinig Dia na Dhia féine
na broinn mar gha ngeil-ghréine
an uimhir do bhaoi na bruinn
gur dhuinigh mar chnaoi i gcrobhuing.[4]

God in his divinity came to her womb as a bright sunbeam, and became man the while he was in her womb, as a nut in its cover.

iv. Aodh mac Conchonnacht Ó Ruanadha (*c.1602*), working perhaps in County Down:

Toirrcheas tharla dar siair mar sin
ar dtiall ó thoil;
fagháil a mic i gcéill nír chuir
mar ghréin tre ghloin.

Thus did her child come to the Virgin of his own will; how she received him coming as a sunbeam through glass she told no man.[5]

However, the second and third of these examples can be set aside. They make no reference to glass, even if they derive from this image. But the first example is of special interest, because it predates instances in many other vernaculars, as we shall see.

In medieval Welsh the theme occurs at least six times. What seems to be the oldest example comes from a poem by Gruffudd Fychan ap Gruffudd ab Ednyfed (*fl. c.*1320? after 1373?) of Anglesey:

> Morwyn vu ueir uwyn o vywn hundy — gwydyr
> yw gwyw dal mab duw vry
> morwyn gynno hynn gein hy
> mirein wawt morwyn wedy.[6]

> A virgin was gentle Mary in a bower of glass, fit to receive the son of God on high, a virgin fair and brave before this, and (noble praise) a virgin after.

These lines are paralleled in medieval English and Latin lyric, which often represent the Virgin as a romance heroine.[7] But the transformation of the glass window into a bower seems to have no parallel. Closer to the conventional image are lines on the Annunciation in a poem (quoted in the previous chapter) by Iolo Goch.

> Yr ysbryd atad, gennad gynnes,
> Efo â chwegair a'th feichioges,
> A Duw o fewn aeth yn dy fynwes
> Fal yr â drwy'r gwydr y terydr tes.[8]

> The spirit to you, a gentle messenger, made you conceive with a sweet word. God entered within your breast as sunshine's augers pass through glass.

A third passage comes from a praise-poem to the Trinity by Gruffudd Llwyd (*fl. c.*1380–1410) of Llangadfan, fourteen miles west of Welshpool, Powys.

Magwyr lân, mygr oleuni,
Mawr yr ymddengys i mi
O len lefn hoywdrefn hydraul,
O wydr hirion belydr haul;
A'r llen a'r dröell honno
Yn gyfan achlân ei chlo.
Haws fu i'r un Duw no hyn
Ym mynwes gwyndw meinwyn
Anfon ei ysbryd iawnfaeth
I Fair, fel rhoi mab ar faeth ... [9]

Great does the blessed enclosure appear to me in the smooth neatly-made delicate sheet, the bright radiance in the glass of long beams of sunlight; and the sheet and that turning is complete and entire in its composition. It was easier than this for the one God to send his nurturing spirit into the bosom of a fair slender shapely body, to Mary, like giving a boy to foster.

From the fifteenth century comes an instance in an anonymous Marian poem (cited in the previous chapter) on the Virgin and her parents, in the style of Hywel Swrdwal (*fl. c.*1430–60).

Bu Fair, o'r gair yn ddi-gêl,
Yn feichiog, o nef uchel.
Mal yr haul y molir hon
Drwy ffenestr wydr i'r ffynnon.
Yr un modd, iawnrhodd anrheg,
Y daeth Duw at famaeth deg.[10]

Mary was with child by the word without concealment, from high heaven. She is praised as sunlight reaching the fountain through the glass of a window; just so did God come to the fair foster-mother, a fair gift, a present.

About the same time the topos features in a poem by Ieuan ap Rhydderch (*fl. c.*1430–70), owner of estates near Lampeter and Aberystwyth in West Wales:

hoiw Fab Duw aeth yn hyfedr
i'th fru fair ddawnair ddinydr
fel haul wybr byw-lwybr baladr
drwy ffenestr wauad-restr wydr.[11]

God's excellent son went most nimbly into your womb, Mary,
a word swift and full of grace, like the sun of heaven, a ray's
living path, through a glass window in glorious array.

The comment on these lines by Jasper Gryffyth (d. 1614),
the zealous Protestant cleric who transcribed what is now
Bangor, University of Wales, MS Gwyneddon 3, is worth
noting. He made his views on other poems clear with such
Latin marginal comments as 'The vain opinion of the
Papists', 'A fable', 'The ignorance of the times in which
this was first written, especially in theology.' But on the
above passage he commented in Welsh, 'It would be a pity
to lose this poem for the sake of this excellent verse',
followed by the lines,

Lumine solari nescit vitrum violari
Nec vitrum sole, nec virgo puerpera prole.[12]

Yet this couplet is medieval, despite its Protestant context.
It derives from the circle of St Anselm of Canterbury
(1033–1109), as discussed below. So the Bangor manuscript shows a curious encounter in Wales of the New
Learning and the Old. A final Welsh instance of the topos
comes from a Marian poem (quoted above) by Hywel ap
Dafydd ab Ieuan ap Rhys (*fl. c.*1450–80), poet to the earls
of Pembroke at Raglan Castle, Monmouthshire:

myned val manay o des
vn dyw vyn yn dy vynwes
yn dri gwisgi lle gwasgaf
drw wydr hayl belydr haf
ay eni n vab ay enw n fwyn
ywch wen vair achwi n vorwyn.[13]

The one God passed, a nimble three, like spots of sunshine

into your bosom, a place most confined; the beams of the summer sun through glass. And he was born a boy and for you, holy Mary, was called beloved, while you remained a virgin.

There is also a reference in Cornish to the sunbeam through glass (a reference here provided by Professor Brian Murdoch of Stirling). In the fifteenth-century miracle play *Beunans Meriasek* 'The Life of Meriadoc', Teudar, the pagan king of Cornwall, is putting arguments against the Virgin Birth. St Meriadoc (a seventh-century bishop of Vannes, on the south coast of Brittany), who is on a missionary journey to Cornwall, is refuting them. So Teudar says,

> erbyn reson yv in beys,
> heb hays gorryth thymo creys
> bones flogh vyth concevijs
> in breys benen.

Against reason is it in the world, without a man's seed, believe me, that a child should ever be conceived in a woman's womb.

Meriadoc replies,

> avel hovle der weder a
> heb y terry del wylsta
> indella crist awartha
> a thuth in breys maris.

As sun goes through glass without breaking it, as thou seest, so Christ above went into Mary's womb.[14]

Murdoch notes that the Latin loan *concevijs* points to a learned origin for the lines. The likely source is the confrontation of Christian and Jew in John Bromyard's *Summa praedicantium*, as argued below.

There is no shortage of examples in vernacular literature other than Celtic. But one point must be emphasized, as it brings out special aspects of the Celtic instances. In Middle English the examples refer more or less clearly to Christ's birth, not his conception. This fact has not been grasped by all Anglicists, who have been misled by instances in art, despite the explicit statements of Aquinas and others that Mary remained a perfect virgin even after Christ's birth, the baby having, as it were, passed through his mother's body as if his body were immaterial. The idea is fundamental to what seems to be the earliest example of the motif (of the early thirteenth century), in a translation of the hymn *Stabat iuxta Christi crucem* on a stray leaf (now in the Bodleian Library) from St Werburgh's Abbey, Chester. The poem likens Christ's resurrection to his birth:

> For swa glem glidis thurh the glas
> of thinë bodi born he was,
> and thurh the halë thurh he glad.

> For he was born of your body as a ray of light passes through glass, and he glided through the intact tomb.[15]

Other examples can be found in the thirteenth-century Harley Lyrics, the Thornton Manuscript, Lydgate, the so-called 'N-Town' cycle of mystery plays, and elsewhere: a final instance occurs as late as 1647, in the *Noble Numbers* of Robert Herrick.

> As sunbeams pierce the glass, and streaming in,
> No crack or schism leave i' th' subtle skin:
> So the divine hand worked, and brake no thread,
> But, in a mother, kept a maidenhead.[16]

In French early examples of it (some secular) occur in the Anglo-Norman poems of William Adgar, writing in the late twelfth century at Barking, Essex; in *Cligés*, written in 1176 by Chrétien de Troyes; in *Queste de Saint Graal* (*c*.1225); the work of Huon le Roi (*c*.1250) of Cambrai, mentioned in the previous chapter; the poems of Rutebeuf (*fl*. 1250–80); and many later writers. In French renaissance poetry it makes a surprise appearance in Marot, as also

Ronsard, who uses it to praise the purity of Marguerite de Navarre (1492–1549), grandmother of Henry IV of France. In the seventeenth century it remained popular with such French spiritual writers at Bérull, Bourgoing, Lessius, Olier, and Pierre Camus. In Provençal the topos appears slightly later than it does in French. It is used by Folquet de Lunel, born near Montpellier, active until 1284; by his contemporary Peire de Corbian, born near Bordeaux; and other writers.[17]

In Middle High German it appears as early as the late eleventh century in a manuscript later in the possession of the Premonstratensian house at Arnstein, in the Rhineland. It also features in the poetry of Walther von der Vogelweide (*c*.1170–*c*.1230), Heinrich von Lauffenberg (d. 1466), and many others. Besides German examples Meiss notes a Dutch one, from a fifteenth-century hymn.[18]

In Italian the figure is put to secular use in a love poem by Giacomo da Lentini (*fl.* 1233–40), court official of Frederick II and founder of the Sicilian school of love lyrics. He used it in a sonnet (a form he may actually have invented) to answer the question he poses himself: how could the image of his beloved have passed through his eyes to his heart? (In this he resembles Chrétien de Troyes.) The Marian use of the topos occurs in *Laude di Cortona* of *c*.1260 and (a famous example) in Tasso's minor poetry. Another exuberant instance may be mentioned here, in the humanist Latin of the Neapolitan poet Jacopo Sannazaro (*c*.1456–1530), in his *De partu Virginis*, described as an 'ambitious attempt at a Christian epic'.[19]

In Spanish poetry the figure appears in *Loores de Nuestra Señora* by Gonzalo de Berceo (*c*.1195–*c*.1265) working in La Rioja, to the west of Navarre; in the *Cantigas* of Alfonso X (1221–84); in Spanish prose, in book two of *Libro de los estados* by Alfonso's nephew, Juan Manuel (1282–1348), and in the Spanish version of the *Elucidarium* of 'Honorius of Autun'. In Catalan it appears in *Vita Christi* (translated into Spanish in 1496) by Françesch Eiximenis. In later Spanish it appears in the work of Gómez Manrique (d. 1490), Íñigo de Mendoza (d. *c*.1507), Juan de Padilla (d.

1520) of the Seville Charterhouse, Luis de León (d. 1591), St John of the Cross, Lope de Vega, and Calderón (who treats it with baroque energy). It figures too in the work of the post-medieval Portuguese poets Agostiño da Cruz and Fernao Alvarez, and the prose writers Sousa de Macedo and Manoel Bernardes. So the Irish instance in Donnchadh Mór Ó Dálaigh takes its place with those of other European poets of the thirteenth century and earlier. Though used by twentieth-century Spanish and Catalan poets, its last appearance as a serious theological concept must be in *Nuevo Ripalda en la Nueva España* (Jérez, 1951), p. 22. This is the thirty-fifth edition of the famous catechism by the Jesuit writer Jerónimo Ripalda. It has a curious history. It first appeared at Burgos in 1591, and was soon translated into Irish by Flaithrí Ó Maol Chonaire or Florence Conry (1560–1629), a Franciscan exile at Salamanca. The Jérez edition sees the work addressed to the unusual circumstances of Franco's Spain.[20] With it, professional theologians bid farewell to the topos.

As far as examples in art are concerned, the earliest one mentioned by standard authorities is at Dijon, in Broederlam's *Annunciation* of 1394–9. It also appears in representations of the Annunciation in the *Très riches heures* of the Duc de Berry; a painting by the master of Flémalle in the Mérode Collection; and paintings by Jan van Eyck in the cathedral of St Bavo at Gent, and in Washington.[21] So, at the same time as poets in the Celtic languages were quoting this theme, it was being used in some of the most sophisticated art of the entire Middle Ages.

What are the origins of this long-lived topos? Here, very strangely, it seems a full account has never been written. One can see why. An exact theologian would not use this image of Christ's conception (his birth is another matter). It might suggest Christ did not take the flesh of his mother, but passed through her (in the coarse phrase of the Paulician heretics of seventh-century Armenia) 'like water through a pipe'.[22] What the following sets out to show is that the theme seems to have originated amongst North African Christians, since the oldest and most influential

text for it occurs in a sermon, falsely attributed to St
Augustine (354–430), which begins *Sanctus hic cum declinat*
and contains the passage:

> Solis radius specular penetrat, et soliditatem eius insensibili
> subtilitate pertraiicit; et videtur intrinsecus qui extat extrinse-
> cus. Nec cum ingreditur dissipat, nec cum egreditur violat;
> quia et ingressu et egressu eius specular integrum perseverat.
> Specular ergo non rumpit radius solis; integritatem Virginis
> ingressus aut egressus vitiare poterat veritatis?[23]

> A sunbeam goes through a pane of glass, and pierces its
> matter with imperceptible subtlety; and what is visible
> outside is seen within. It scatters nothing when it goes in and
> breaks nothing when it comes out, because on its entry and
> exit the pane stays whole. The sunbeam thus does not break
> the pane of glass; could the entry and exit of the truth harm
> the purity of the Virgin?

The sermon abounds in oddities. Its prolixity is marked by
vivid, abrupt expressions; recondite vocabulary; bizarre
etymologies; unfamiliar versions of Bible texts; and
polemics against Jews and Manichaeans. These provide
strong evidence for a North African provenance of the
fifth or sixth century, though an attribution to St Augustine must, of course, be ruled out. The description here of
the pane of glass (*specular*, a Late Latin word, used by
Tertullian) clearly shows Mary remained a virgin after
both Christ's conception and his birth.

This strange 'African' sermon, first published (from an
eleventh-century copy at Monte Cassino) in 1836, was
little known in the Middle Ages. Yet its ideas gained
enormous popularity, bceause they were amongst the
sources of a second sermon spuriously attributed to St
Augustine. This latter sermon, beginning *Legimus sanctum
Moysen populo dei*, was written probably in sixth- or
seventh-century Italy (or perhaps France). Barré regarded
the text as coming either from the circle of St Caesarius of
Arles (*c.*470–543), who spent periods at Ravenna and
Rome, or that of Gregory the Great (*c.*540–604). In any

case, it incorporates the above passage from our North African sermon wholesale. The influence of the 'Legimus' sermon was soon reinforced by the incorporation of much of it, including the 'Solis radius' passage, into a third sermon, a Marian one beginning *Exhortatur nos dominus deus* spuriously attributed to St Ildefonsus of Toledo (c.610–67). but probably written in Italy in the earlier seventh century.[24] This was also extremely popular in the Middle Ages.

Barré has made clear the scissors-and-paste nature of these two later sermons, as well as the modest intellectual endowments of their unknown authors. Yet they enjoyed an influence out of all proportion to their merits, not least in giving European circulation to the metaphor of sunbeam and glass from their North African source. In Britain and Ireland this source had special influence, because it was included (from the 'Legimus' sermon) as an Advent reading in the Sarum Breviary.[25] The importance of this is hard to exaggerate. It is thus likely that the main source here for Welsh and Irish poets (but not the Cornish one) was the liturgy. It is also worth noting that the treatment of this point by such scholars as Norton-Smith and Greene is unsatisfactory. The first quotes the 'Solis radius' passage from 'sermon iii' of St Ildefonsus; but 'iii' is his error for 'xiii', and the text is in any case not by Ildefonsus. As for Greene, he states that 'the most authoritative use of the figure' was that of St Augustine, quoting the 'Solis radius' passage from the Sarum Breviary.[26] But Augustine has nothing to do with it.

If Anglicists can err, so can Latinists. Barré showed the 'Exhortatur' sermon was written probably in the seventh century. Yet some years previously Díaz y Díaz had described it as late, seeing the image of the sunbeam through glass as 'a consequence of the Marian movements of the eleventh and twelfth centuries, appearing as such in MS Soissons 123 (114) of the twelfth century, and Munich Clm. 9727, of the fifteenth century'.[27] Art historians also nod. Hirn describes the figure as occurring 'from the start of the ninth century'. The treatment by Millard Meiss of medieval Latin texts is also unsatisfactory.[28]

It is thanks to Barré that we can now push the origins of the theme right back to the sixth or even fifth century. One early example of its influence is of special interest. Although Ildefonsus did not write the 'Exhortatur' sermon, it was known in Toledo in his time, because it is one of the sermons in the *Homiliae Toletanae* collection of that date. The sunbeam theme even figures in a verse by St Eugenius of Toledo (*c.*600–57), Bishop of Toledo immediately before Ildefonsus. Presumably Eugenius took the idea from the copy of the sermon still extant in *Homiliae Toletanae* or from its exemplar.

> Ut Phoebus specular intrans corrumpere nescit,
> sic Christum generans virgo Maria manet.[29]

> As the sun entering a pane of glass cannot mar it, so Mary conceiving Christ remains a virgin.

This epigram, typical of the Latin culture of Visigothic Spain, helped spread the figure of the sunbeam, since (as Raby points out) Eugenius was 'a prolific versifier, much read in England and by the Carolingians'.[30] So much is shown in a monograph, based on the study of 180 manuscripts, by Y.-F. Riou on the circulation and influence of Eugenius's complete *Libellus diversi carminis*, in which the above verse appears.[31]

The epigram by Eugenius can be compared with the Latin couplet, probably by an associate of St Anselm, in the sixteenth-century Gwyneddon manuscript at Bangor. Sir Richard Southern called the figure of glass and sunbeam 'a simile much used in the school of Anselm', where Jewish objections to Christian belief were a matter of concern. This particular Anselmian couplet was given wide circulation by *Summa praedicantium*, a handbook for preachers compiled in the second quarter of the fourteenth century by John Bromyard, a Dominican. He used it (in the section 'Maria', article 17) in the same way as Anselm's disciple, as the response to a Jew's objection to the Virgin Birth (even through by Bromyard's time Jews no longer existed in England, Edward I having expelled them). But in fifteenth-century manuscripts the Jew's verse is placed in the mouth of a heretic, as follows:

Nunquam natura mutare solet sua iura,
Ut virgo pareret quin virginitate careret.[32]

Nature is not wont to change its laws, that a virgin should give birth without losing her virginity.

This Anselmian dialogue must have been familiar to the unknown author of *Beunans Meriasek*, where the pagan Teudar is the antagonist. Because Hans Walther collected examples of these couplets from manuscripts in Paris, Basel, Munich, and Prague, it is possible for us to see how the Cornish priest who wrote *Beunans Meriasek* and the Elizabethan parson Jasper Gryffyth were, in their use of them, part of a truly European mode of expression.[33]

Other Latin texts show how common the figure was in the Middle Ages. Meiss quotes it from what he took to be the work of St Bernard (1090–1153), on how Mary remained virgin after Christ's conception and birth.

Sicut splendor solis vitrum absque laesione perfundit et pene-trat eiusque *soliditatem insensibili subtilitate pertraicit nec cum ingreditur, violat nec, cum egreditur, dissipat*: sic Dei verbum, splendor Patris, virginum habitaculum adiit et inde clauso utero prodiit.[34]

Just as the sun's splendour leaves intact the glass it penetrates and goes through, passing through its matter with an imperceptible subtlety, neither breaking it as it enters nor scattering it as it leaves: so the Word of God, the Splendour of the Father, gained access to the virgin dwelling-place and thereafter left the womb intact.

But the words in italic are not original to St Bernard. They are from our 'African' sermon of the fifth or sixth century. Nor is the text itself by Bernard. It does not appear in the microfiche concordance of his work. Meiss quotes it from

Salzer; Salzer quotes it from Stamm. One wonders who the real author was. Quoting Meiss, Carol Purtle speaks of Bernard's 'use' of this topos, which cannot be right.[35] A scholar with access to the texts may be able to inform us who the real author is here.

An early example of the sunbeam through glass topos in a hymn occurs in the work of Adam of St Victor (*c*.1110–*c*.1180), a (Breton?) monk of the Abbey of St Victor, near Paris. In his sequence *Splendor patris et figura*, sung at his abbey on 30 December, he declares:

> Si crystallus sit humecta
> Atque soli sit obiecta,
> Scintillat igniculum:
> Nec crystallus rumpitur,
> Nec in partu solvitur
> Pudoris signaculum.[36]

> If glass is moistened and placed in the sun, it sparkles. The glass is not broken, and the seal of purity is not broken.

The same figure occurs in a hymn of Alexander Neckam (1157–1217), teacher at Dunstable and Paris, and from 1213 Abbot of Cirencester; the anonymous thirteenth-century *Salve, porta crystallina* and (familiar in the manuscript and printed massbooks of Seville) *Novis cedunt vetera*; and the *Revelations* of St Bridget of Sweden (*c*.1302–73). In her first vision, Christ told her, *Quia sicut Sol vitrum ingrediendo non laedit, sic nec virginitas Virginis in assumptione humanitatis meae corrupta est*, 'For as the sun penetrating a glass window does not damage it, the virginity of the Virgin is not spoiled by my assumption of human form.'[37] (This Latin version soon appeared in Swedish: *i iomfrunna inälwe swa som solin skinande gynom renasten sten älli glas*, 'into the Virgin's bosom like the sun passing through a transparent stone or glass'.) The theme remained common in hymns to the end of the Middle Ages.[38]

A full account of the sunbeam through glass would provide material for a monograph, particularly if it included material from Eastern Europe and elsewhere. But enough has been done to show what such an account would look like, and how it would include some of the most famous names in European literature and art. It would, however, also include poetry in Irish, Welsh, and Cornish, each using this ancient Latin metaphor for its own purposes to honour the Virgin and her Son.

After the sunbeam through glass, the Trinity in the Blessed Virgin's womb. This theme is widespread in medieval literature and art. The Dutch scholar Johan Huizinga (1872–1945) gave a characteristic description of it:

> In the fifteenth century, people used to keep statuettes of the Virgin, of which the body opened and showed the Trinity within. The inventory of the treasure of the Dukes of Burgundy makes mention of one made of gold inlaid with gems.

Huizinga goes on to mention another such statue seen at the Carmelite house in Paris by Jean Gerson (1363–1429), Chancellor of Paris University. Gerson, who saw in the statue 'neither beauty, nor devotion' but rather a way of breeding error and profanity, did more than just criticize it. He had it destroyed.[39]

Hirn likewise referred to the theme, mentioning the celebrated *vierge ouvrante* (with doors at the front) in the Church of Notre-Dame du Mur at Morlaix, on the north coast of Brittany, and other such statues in the Louvre and at Lyon. Hirn also quoted the lines *Salve mater pietatis, / et totius trinitatis / nobile triclinium*, 'Hail, mother of piety and noble couch of all the Trinity' from a sequence by Adam of St Victor (d. *c*.1180), which were so famous that they appear below the *Annunciation* by Fra Angelico in the Church of San Marco, Florence.[40]

Huizinga and Hirn between them suggest how well known this motif was in medieval France, Burgundy, and Italy. Other evidence for it occurs in English, Welsh, and Spanish sources, as well as in medieval Latin texts from various European countries. Yet it is in Irish that we find the most remarkable literary expression of it, in the following poem by Donnchadh Mór Ó Dálaigh.

Buime trír máthair mhic Dé;
go roibh linn i ló an fhínné
 a radhalta an rí neamhdha
 banaltra thrí dtighearna.

A n-altrom nír dheacair dhí
trí branáin chláir na cruinne
 aobhdha an triar a trí dhalta
 dá riar do bhí an bhanaltra.

Buime an trír-sin Muire mhór
dá n-altrom do bhí am bhanógh
 triur i n-aoncholainn amh-áin
 nó gur aonchrobhaing anbháil.

Ag inghin an fhuilt leabhair
maith do uair a oileamhain
 a hathair i n-ucht Mhuire
 athaidh i gcurp cholluidhe.

An mac do b'fheirr-de i-se
dá oileamhain aicei-se;
 an rí caránta ar a cígh
 baránta í don airdrígh.

An treas cnú don chrobhaing ghlan
teachtaire a hucht an Athar
 fa hé a ionad a huicht-se
 Spiorad Dé ar a diadhaicht-se.

Toircheas na hóighe is é an fáidh
aice do fhuair a thógbháil;
 ag so an tí do fhóir orainn
 trí cno óir haonchrobhaing.

Triur as ghoire gaol di-se,
triur do hoileadh aicei-se,
 trí leannáin ler luigh Muire
 beangáin fhuil a haonmhuine.

Triur i n-a dtrí daltaibh dhi
trí meic ochta na hóighe;
   gach rí dhíbh ruinn-ne dá roinn
   trí rígh na cruinne an chrobhuing.

Trí heochracha mhúir Muire
trí tobair na trócuire,
   rí 'n-a aonduine ós gach fhior,
   trí aoghuire dom fheitheamh.

Trí dhalta Mhuire móire
toircheas bronn na banóighe;
   an tí tharla ar úide gach fhir
   trí gabhla dhúin an Dúilimh.

An triur-soin ón tigh neamhdha
an Tríonóid, ar dtighearna;
   neach do bhí 'n-a bhráthair di
   is í a mháthair 's a mhuime.[41]

The mother of God's son is the nurse of three; nurse of three lords, may her great child, the heavenly king, be with us on the Day of Judgement.

It was not difficult for her to nurse them, three champions of the world's chessboard. Her three foster-sons are a beautiful three, their nurse was providing for them.

Great Mary was nurse of these three, the Virgin reared them, three in one single body, so that they were one single magnificent cluster.

Well was he nursed by the girl of the long smooth hair, Mary's own Father in her bosom, for a while in an earthly body.

The Son by whom she was exalted was being nursed by her; the crowned king on her breast, she was the high-king's protector.

The third nut of the holy cluster, a messenger on behalf of the Father, the Spirit of God: because of her piety, her breast was his place.

The Virgin's offspring is the prophet, he was fed by her; here is the one who saved us: three golden nuts from a single cluster.

Three who are closer kin to her, three who were nursed by her, three lovers Mary lay with, shoots which are of a single shrub.

Three who were her three foster-sons, three beloved sons of the Virgin; each king of them is shared with us, the three kings of the Universe are the cluster.

Three keys of Mary's castle, three founts of mercy, a king who alone is above every man, three shepherds to guard me.

Three foster-sons of great Mary, offspring of the Virgin's womb; the one who has attracted the attention of every man, three pillars of the Creator's stronghold.

This three from the heavenly mansion is the Trinity, our lord; he who was her brother, it is she who is his mother and nurse.

Donnchadh speaks in this curious, tender poem of the Father, Son, and Holy Spirit as 'three in one single body', and 'three foster-sons of great Mary, offspring of the Virgin's womb'. The reference to the Trinity in the Virgin's womb could hardly be clearer: the poem is Irish evidence for the tradition described by Huizinga and Hirn. The continued copying of the poem, and the line *buime trír is í 'na hóigh* by one of two poets named Aonghus Ó Dálaigh (of about 1600), suggest poem and tradition alike remained familiar in Ireland even after the Middle Ages.[42] In the rest of Catholic Europe the devotion seems to have faded with the reforms of the Council of Trent.

Yet the link between Donnchadh's poem and the cult of the Trinity in the Virgin's womb has not had proper emphasis. O'Dwyer, for example, glosses the poem with numerous medieval statements on the relationship of the Virgin to different persons of the Trinity. The comments he assembles are of interest. But none actually mentions the Trinity in the Virgin's womb.[43] What follows has thus been written to show that Donnchadh's poem is part of a specific popular European devotion, and can be paralleled repeatedly in the poetry and art of Britain and the Continent.

Evidence from beyond Ireland also casts light on which of two poets called Donnchadh Mór Ó Dálaigh wrote our poem. The first, 'a poet who never was and never will be surpassed', died in 1244 and was buried at Boyle Abbey, north of Roscommon; the second, active before about 1400, lived at Finavarra in County Clare, between Galway and the Burren. Although references to the Trinity in the Virgin's womb occur in twelfth-century Latin, no instance in art or vernacular literature seems to predate the fourteenth century. This strengthens the case for attribution to the later Donnchadh. In stanza five the loanword *baránta* from Anglo-Norman *warant* (where the sense is the original one 'protector', though Irish dictionaries do not recognize this) also favours the later Donnchadh, as other instances of *baránta* date from much later than 1244, while even the earliest in English (in the Midlands prose text *Seinte Margarete*) cannot be much older than 1250.[44]

Turning from Ireland to Britain, we find the two most interesting literary examples of the theme are in Welsh. Of these, the earlier appears in a Marian poem beginning *Doeth y'th etholes Iesu*. This poem, now attributed again to Iolo Goch (*c.*1320–*c.*1400), is in the formal archaic style of the *Gogynfeirdd* or Welsh court poets of the twelfth to early fourteenth centuries.

Yr ysbryd atad, gennad gynnes,
Efo â chwegair a'th feichioges,
A Duw o fewn aeth yn dy fynwes
Fal yr â drwy'r gwydr y terydr tes.
Megis bagad o rad rodres,
Tair cneuen gwisgi, tri y tröes
Yn Dad, drwy gariad y rhagores,
Yn fab gwyn arab araf cynnes,
Yn ysbryd glendyd, glandeg armes.[45]

The spirit to you, gentle messenger, made you conceive with a sweet word. God entered within your breast as sunshine's augers pass through glass. Like a cluster of blessed splendour, three ripe nuts, turned as three [persons] into the Father in love excelled, into the blessed, pleasant, dear, gentle Son; into the Spirit of Holiness, fair and holy prophecy.

The description above of the Trinity as 'three ripe nuts' is curiously like Donnchadh's 'three nuts of gold'. *Cnú* 'nut' is a favourite endearment of Irish poetry, but not of Welsh, though *y gneuen wisgi* appears in another poem by Iolo, about a journey to Scotland (as Richard II's ambassador) of Ieuan Trefor, Bishop of St Asaph 1395–1410.[46] Perhaps the expression shows Irish influence on Iolo.

The second instance of the motif occurs in a fifteenth-century poem (already quoted) in the style of Hywel Swrdwal, beginning *Archwn i Fair a bair byd.*

> Da fu'r fun, eiddun addef
> Dan ei chnawd, dwyn i chwi nef;
> Dwyn ei mab o'i daioni,
> A dwyn ei thad a wnaeth hi.
> Bu'r Drindod, is rhod yr haul,
> A'i [h]annedd yn y wennaul.[47]

Good was the maid, desirable dwelling, she bore heaven to you within her flesh; from her goodness she bore her Son and bore her Father who made her. The Trinity below the sun's orb had its dwelling in the bright radiance.[48]

The last two lines here are based on Psalm 18:6 (AV 19:4), which the Douay Bible renders 'He hath set his tabernacle in the sun.' As the Virgin is often called 'the sun', the verse is frequently applied to her acceptance of the Trinity at the Annunciation.[49] So it is more than just a pretty allusion by the poet. It shows scriptural learning.

English evidence for the cult of the Trinity in the Virgin's womb will not keep us long. It is more varied than that from Ireland and Wales, and includes poetry, drama, and art. But the literary instances are less impressive than those in the Celtic languages. No doubt much was lost at the Reformation. One early allusion occurs in the opening lines of a song to the Virgin perhaps by William of Shoreham (*c*.1325), parish priest of Chart in Kent.

> Marye, maide, milde and fre
> Chambre of the Trinite.[50]

A fifteenth-century instance comes from an anonymous poem to the Virgin from manuscripts now in London, Oxford, Cambridge, Edinburgh, and Dublin libraries.

> Heil, welle of witt and of merci!
> Heil, that bare Jesu, Goddes sone!
> Heil, tabernacle of the trynyte,
> *Funde preces ad filium!*[51]

Other evidence for the theme occurs in the drama cycle *Ludus Coventriae*, which was put together in its present form about 1440, perhaps at Lincoln (not Coventry, despite its title). In play 11, on the 'Salutation and Conception', there occurs this stage direction:

> Here the holy gost discendit with iij bemys to our lady; the sone of the godhed nest with iij bemys to the holy gost; the fadyr godly with iij bemys to the sone; and so entre all three to here bosom.[52]

The theme also figures in English art. Near Stamford is the curiously-named village of Barnack (?linked, aptly for a quarrying place, to Old Cornish *bern* 'heap'), with a fifteenth-century sculpture of the Annunciation which in part matches the above stage directions.[53] Perhaps the sculptor, working in the Diocese of Lincoln, saw the play. As for the *vierges ouvrantes*, although (as we shall see below) their evidence should be used critically, the various Continental images had at least one English sister, at Durham. This revered image, 'Our Lady of Bolton'

(= Boulton), was on solemn occasions venerated by the laity, above all on Good Friday, when the statue would be opened, the cross of gold within would be seen, and the faithful in the cathedral would pass before it, kneeling one by one. The image occupies a special place in *Rites of Durham*, the famous recollections (written long after the Dissolution by someone who lived through it) of monastic life in the cathedral priory:

> Every principall daie the said immage was opened that every man might se pictured within her, the father, the sonne, and the holy ghost, most curiouslye and fynely gilted.[54]

Other evidence for the theme of the Trinity in the Virgin's womb occurs in a carol by James Ryman, a Canterbury Franciscan writing about 1492. His application to the Virgin of the rare word *tryclyn* borrows sacred wit from Adam of St Victor's *triclinium*, both 'a chamber' and 'a couch for three'.

> O tryclyn of the Trinite,
> Replete with alle diuinite,
> O flowre of alle uirginitie,
>   *Ora pro nobis.*[55]

In the rest of Europe are many references in Latin texts, beginning with Adam of St Victor, to the Virgin's womb as 'chamber' or 'temple' of the Trinity. These references have been methodically listed in a German Marian encyclopedia. Amongst twelfth- and thirteenth-century texts there listed is a treatise by Hugh of St Victor; *Libellus de corona Virginis* by pseudo-Ildefonsus; a sermon, by Hélinard de Froidmont, on the Assumption; a commentary by St Albert the Great on St Luke's Gospel; a sermon by St Bonaventura on the Assumption; and St Thomas Aquinas's commentary on the Angelic Salutation.[56] There must also be many references to the devotion in medieval French, German, Italian, and other Continental vernaculars. Further work on this could be done by scholars with

access to appropriate libraries. A passage from a French
Christmas sermon quoted by Huizinga (who calls it proof
of heresy) shows what can be found:

> quant pour les pécheurs se voust en vous herbergier le Père,
> le Filz et le Saint-Esprit; par quoy vous estes la chambre de
> toute la Trinité;

> when the Father, the Son, and the Holy Spirit deigned to take
> up their abode in you, Mary, for the sake of sinners, whereby
> you are the chamber of the whole Trinity.[57]

There is also evidence for the theme in medieval Spanish
poetry. An early instance appears in an expanded version
of the *Ave Maria* by Pero López de Ayala (1332–?1407),
statesman, soldier, historian, and prisoner of war:

> Contigo Trinidat allí fue ayuntada
> La corte celestial en ti fizo morada:
> Madre de Dios, Esposa, Fija fueste llamada:
> Bien así de los santos fueste profectizada.[58]

> The Trinity was there united with you, the court of heaven
> made its dwelling in you; God's Mother, Wife, and Daughter
> were you called; well were you prophesied thus amongst the
> saints.

A further instance occurs in a poem by Alfonso Álvarez
Villasandino (*c.*1350–?1425), born near Burgos, who spent
his life as poet-for-hire at the Castilian court:

> Generosa, muy fermosa,
> Syn mansilla Virgen santa,
> Virtuosa, poderosa,
> De quien Lucifer se espanta;
> Tanta fue la tu gran omildat
> Que toda la Trinidat
> En ty se ençierra, se canta.[59]

> Generous, most beautiful, holy Virgin without spot; virtuous,
> mighty, dreaded by Lucifer; so great was your humility, that
> the whole Trinity is enclosed and praised in you.

A final example occurs in the *Cantiga en loores de Santa Marya de Guadalupe* by Pero Vélez de Guevara (d. 1420), nephew of one noble poet (López de Ayala) and uncle of another (Íñigo López de Mendoza, marqués de Santillana).

Quando al angel dexiste
Sancta fue aquella ora,
Ecce ancilla, señora,
Dios e omne conçebiste ...
Señora so cuyo manto
Cupieron çielos y tierra
En la trynidad s'ençierra
Padro, Fijo, Spiritu Santo.[60]

When you said (holy was that hour) *ecce ancilla* to the angel, Lady, you conceived God and Man ... Lady, beneath your mantle there fitted the heavens and the earth, Father, Son, and Holy Spirit enclosed in the Trinity.

These examples in Spanish prove Donnchadh's poem is no oddity. The theme is almost a commonplace of medieval European poetry, even if often expressed in a heterodox way; as Herrán remarks, the Spanish poets sometimes confuse the fact that the Incarnation was the work of the whole Trinity with the strange notion that the Virgin Mary conceived the Trinity. It was thus that the idea of the Virgin as temple or dwelling place of the Trinity, taught by some of the greatest of the Church's teachers and hymn-writers, was twisted into bizarre errors that would have dismayed them.

Yet the most spectacular aspect of this theme is found not in poetry, but in sculpture, in the *vierges ouvrantes* mentioned above. These statues led to real accusations of heresy, both in the Middle Ages and later, as it was maintained that they showed the Blessed Virgin as having conceived not simply the Son, but the whole Trinity. They were thus destroyed in great numbers in the sixteenth century, and few genuine ones survive. The Spanish scholar Manuel Trens said he knew only of some two dozen. Many of those in modern collections are nineteenth-century forgeries.

Trens discussed the iconography of the *vierge ouvrante* by reference to scriptural texts, some of which would apply to Donnchadh's poem: 'All the glory of the king's daughter is within' of Psalm 44:14 (AV 45:13); 'If a man loves me, he will keep my word, and my Father will love him, and we will come to him and make our home in him' of John 14:23 (in the Navarre Bible); and 'A bundle of myrrh is my beloved to me: he shall abide between my breasts' of Song of Songs 1:12. By 'myrrh' the Fathers of the Church understood the Passion, Death, and Burial of Jesus: hence the figures of the crucified Christ inside many of these statues.[61]

Yet not all *vierges ouvrantes* contain representations of the Trinity. Some open to reveal images of the Joys of the Virgin, or her Sorrows, and even those with the Trinity are not all directly relevant to the present theme. Trens distinguished two kinds of statue of the Virgin containing the Trinity. With the first, doors open from neck to foot of the image of the Virgin to show a representation of the Trinity occupying the whole interior of the image. Trens cited as an example of this the fifteenth-century statue of the *Mare de Deu de la Santíssima Trinitat* at Palau del Vidre in Roussillon, on France's border with Catalonia. The Trinity there appears in the form of the 'Throne of Grace', with God the Father enthroned and holding the Son, crucified, between his hands, and the Holy Spirit shown as a flying dove. Trens noted the same form in the 'Lady of Bolton' described in the Durham *Ritual*.

But it is the second kind of *vierge ouvrante*, in which the Trinity is shown occupying, not the whole body of the Virgin, but her actual womb, which is the exact parallel of our literary texts. These statues are of extreme rarity since they were the ones naturally most open to the charge of heresy. The Carmelite statue seen by Gerson may have been of this kind. The only instance known to this writer is a Spanish one, the Virgin of Buiñondo in an *ermita* or shrine at Vergara, a small Basque town some forty miles west-north-west of Pamplona. The Trinity is revealed in the statue, not by the opening of doors, but by the removal of a panel covering the Virgin's abdomen. The Trinity, a small gold-coloured assemblage, is represented as a Throne of Grace against a blue background covered in gold stars. The Virgin wears a red gown, blue cloak, and a crown; she holds her hands (which have been restored) upwards, palms towards the spectator. The statue, wooden and thirty-six inches high, was dated by Lizarralde to the last third of the fourteenth century, but by Trens to the fifteenth.[62]

Evidence from different countries suggests, therefore, that the theme of Donnchadh's poem is not peculiar to Ireland, but is part of a widespread European tradition which begins with the great Latin writers of the twelfth and thirteenth centuries. In later centuries the devotion spread to art and vernacular literature, both at an elite level (the Carmelite house at Paris, Spanish court poetry, and perhaps the images in the Duke of Burgundy's treasury and at Durham) and a more popular one (*Ludus Coventriae*, the Buiñondo statue). It seems probable the basis for Donnchadh's poem came to Ireland from the Continent with the Latin learning of the Church, rather than via art or vernacular literature. Even though with Donnchadh's poem Irish vernacular tradition, like that of Spain, may have made a heterodox theme of an orthodox one, the sources of the motif are clear enough. If the theme emerged from the 'cauldron of resurrection' of the Irish bards completely Gaelic in manner and expression, it still bears the traces of its Continental origins.

Notes

1. Gray, *Themes*, pp. 101, 258–9.
2. McKenna, *Dán Dé*, pp. xv, 53, 118; cf. O'Dwyer, *Mary*, p. 78.
3. McKenna, *Aithdioghluim*, i, p. 224, ii, p. 133.
4. McKenna, *Dánta*, p. 59; cf. O'Dwyer, *Mary*, p. 195.
5. McKenna, *Aithdioghluim*, i, p. 311, ii, p. 192.
6. Gwenogvryn Evans, col. 1295.
7. Gray, *Themes*, pp. 91–4; Breeze, 'The Virgin Mary and Romance', 144.

8. Johnston, *Gwaith Iolo Goch*, pp. 139–40.
9. Ifor Williams and Thomas Roberts, p. 151.
10. Ibid., p. 96.
11. Ifor Williams, *Gwyneddon 3*, p. 30.
12. Ibid., pp. vii, 350; cf. Greene, p. 356.
13. E. Stanton Roberts, p. 158, emended from Lloyd-Jones, p. 687.
14. Stokes, pp. 48–9; cf. Murdoch, p. 110.
15. Gray, *Themes*, p. 101; Dobson and Harrison, pp. 147, 151.
16. Brook, p. 35; Sisam and Sisam, pp. 166, 190–1; Gray, *Selections*, p. 258.
17. Becker, p. 21; Oroz, pp. 130, 372–4.
18. Salzer, pp. 71–4; Meiss, pp. 175–81; von der Leyen, pp. 136, 742; Sayce, p. 107.
19. Contini, i, p. 76; ii, pp. 15–16; Sparrow and Perosa, p. 157.
20. Rodríguez, pp. 305, 534; Kinkade, p. 113; Manuel, p. 235; Gonzalo de Berceo, pp. 107; Herrán, pp. 365, 498–9; *Las Edades del Hombre*, pp. 401–2.
21. Meiss, pp. 176–8; cf. Madigan, pp. 227–30.
22. Gray, *Themes*, p. 259.
23. Hamman, ii, col. 922.
24. Barré, 'Le sermon', 10–33.
25. R. T. Davies, p. 377; Greene, p. 348.
26. Lydgate, p. 148; Greene, p. 348.
27. Díaz, pp. 280–1.
28. Meiss, 175–81; Hirn, 244; Purtle, 33, n. 60.
29. Vollmer, p. 261.
30. Raby, *Oxford Book of Medieval Latin Verse*, p. 461.
31. Riou, 11–44.
32. Greene, p. 356.
33. Ifor Williams, *Gwyneddon 3*, vii, p. 350.
34. Meiss, 176.
35. Stamm, p. 131; Salzer, p. 74; Meiss, 176; Purtle, 33.
36. Dreves and Blume, i, p. 260; Dagens, 526.
37. Ibid., ii, p. 278; Hirn, pp. 244–5; Meiss, 177.
38. Gray, *Themes*, p. 258, n. 23.
39. Huizinga, *Waning*, p. 151.
40. Raby, *Christian Latin Poetry*, p. 349; Hirn, pp. 229, 379; Gray, *Themes*, p. 237; Baumer, pp. 237–72; Estella, pp. 125–46.
41. McKenna, *Dioghluim Dána*, pp. 29–30.
42. *Dictionary of the Irish Language*, s.v. *tríar*; de Brún, p. 181.
43. O'Dwyer, *Mary*, p. 87–8.
44. McKenna, *Dán Dé*, pp. viii–ix, and his *Dioghluim Dána*, p. 624; Vendryes, *Lexique*, p. 17.
45. Johnston, *Gwaith Iolo Goch*, pp. 139–40.

46. Johnston, *Gwaith Iolo Goch*, p. 284.
47. Ifor Williams and Thomas Roberts, p. 93.
48. Cf. Clancy, *Medieval Welsh Lyrics*, pp. 162.
49. Gray, *Selection*, pp. 101–2.
50. R. T. Davies, pp. 103, 371.
51. Gray, *Selection*, p. 71.
52. Gray, *Themes*, pp. 237–8.
53. Pevsner, p. 209; Coates and Breeze, pp. 322.
54. Gray, *Themes*, p. 237.
55. Ibid., p. 237; Greene, p. 142.
56. Algermissen, coll. 1448–9; Bäumer and Scheffczyk, ii. pp. 233–41.
57. Huizinga, *Herbst*, p. 498.
58. Herrán, p. 354.
59. Ibid., p. 345.
60. Ibid., pp. 354–5.
61. Trens, pp. 481–6, 497–502; Réau, pp. 92–3.
62. Lizarralde, pp. 54–6.

Virgin and Child

The Annunciation and Incarnation lead naturally to the Nativity and images of the Virgin and her Child. The Nativity brings us to a famous thirteenth-century Welsh poem by Madog ap Gwallter (almost certainly a Franciscan friar); the Virgin and Child to poems of veneration, and also to the strange legend of the Instantaneous Harvest on the Flight into Egypt. Altogether, then, varied perceptions of Mary in medieval Wales and Ireland.

First, Madog's poem on Christ's Nativity, *Mab a'n rhodded*, 'A son was given us'.[1] This has been much admired. Often called the 'earliest Christmas carol' in Welsh (though it lacks the refrain of a true carol), its 'freshness' and 'atmosphere of the early Franciscan world' have led to the belief that Madog was a Friar Minor.[2] The fact that Madog's poem shares motifs with thirteenth-century English poems (written probably by friars) strengthens this case, even if the 'Franciscan spirit' did not end in 1300, or lacks precursors before 1200.[3]

The first friary in Wales was founded by 1242.[4] This gives a *terminus a quo* for Madog, since it is agreed he was a friar. His *terminus ad quem* is provided by Cardiff, South Glamorgan Central Library, MS 2.611 (*c.*1275 x 1325), if he is the 'Frater Walensis madocus edeirnianensis' whose Latin hexameters figure there; if not, by the Red Book of Hergest (*c.*1400), the earliest manuscript containing his Welsh poems. Arguments for dating Madog to *c.*1250 on the basis of a statement by Dr John Davies of Mallwyd (*c*.1567–1644), and for considering him a Franciscan, are supported by his apparent knowledge of the Middle English religious text *Sawles Warde*, which was copied by Hereford Franciscans about that time, but which did not circulate much after about 1300.[5]

The date of Madog's career also has implications for English poetry. No separate Middle English poem (Franciscan or otherwise) on the Nativity is known before 1372, when the Norfolk friar John of Grimestone compiled his preaching book.[6] Rosemary Woolf thus assumed nativity lyric was a late form due to the influence of miracle plays, where the Nativity was detached from its liturgical season. But Gray thinks that arguing from such negative evidence, when a 'find' from the thirteenth century might transform the picture, is dangerous.[7] If Madog's poem was written before 1300, as seems the case, it is the 'find' Anglicists have been waiting for. It suggests vernacular nativity lyric existed in Britain at an early date, that it had nothing to do with the drama, and that it was the work of the friars.

Madog's poem on the Nativity has unusual stylistic interest. Despite its alleged simplicity and homeliness, it contains the ancient European paradox of God's humility, of the divine king born in a stable.[8]

Ych ac assen,	Arglwyd pressen,	presseb pieu;
A sopen weir	yn lle kadeir	y'n lliw kadeu.
Pali ny mynn,	nyt vryael gwynn	y gynhynneu;
Yn lle syndal	ygkylch y wal	gwelit carpeu.

An ox and an ass, the Lord of this world, a manger is his; bundle of hay instead of a cradle for our Lord of hosts. No silk he wishes, no splendid fabrics are his for covers: instead of linen about his bedstead, one saw but tatters.[9]

A Franciscan might naturally stress the pathos of the scene.[10] Significantly, it is absent from the Red Book of Talgarth lyric on the Virgin and Child discussed above and below. But in Latin poetry the theme itself is as old as the hymn *Agnoscat omne saeculum* by Venantius Fortunatus (*c*.530–?609), Bishop of Poitiers.

Praesaepe poni pertulit,
Qui lucis auctor exstitit,
Cum patre caelos condidit,
Sub matre pannos induit.[11]

He allowed himself to be laid in a manger; he who, when he
who created the heavens with his Father showed himself
creator of light, is wrapped in swaddling in the arms of his
mother.

Smaragdus (*fl.* 809–19), of Saint-Mihiel-sur-Meuse near
Verdun, expresses the idea more boldly:

Qui totum mundum vestit ornatu, pannis vilibus involvitur
... per quem omnia facta sunt, manus pedesque cunis astrin-
gitur ... cuius coelum sedes est, duri praesepis angustia
continet.

He who adorned the whole universe, is wrapped in mean
swaddling ... he through whom all things were made, is
bound hand and foot in a cradle ... he whose throne is the
heavens, is contained within the narrowness of a roughly-
made crib.[12]

A Middle English snatch puts the theme into three lines,
laying less stress on the paradox, more on the pathos of an
ox's stall as 'royal throne' and on Mary as the one servant
this king has:

Of one stable was his halle,
His kenestol on occe stalle,
Seinte Marie his burnes all.[13]

The verse, written down in the Worcester-Hereford region
*c.*1255–60 in a friars' preaching book (now Cambridge,
Trinity College, MS 323), can be linked with Madog's
poem. Both dwell on the pathos of the Incarnation; both
place delicate emphasis on the Virgin Mary. Madog's
picture of an infant king with silks, splendid fabrics, or
linen, is paralleled by another poem in this Trinity manuscript, on the Three Kings, which declares that the Lord

who made us all wore neither ermine nor grey fur:

> Ne werede he nouther fou ne grey
> The loverd that us alle havet iwroust.[14]

The above topoi thus show sophisticated simplicity. Yet the special tenderness with which Madog treats the Virgin is still worth noting. Later in the poem, describing how the Magi found Jesus in the stable, the images of the royal hall that lacked door and enclosure, and of a divine king who is a baby fed by his mother, maintain the paradox of the Incarnation:

> Y'r ty yd ant,   heb dor, heb gant,   gwynnawc dryssev;
> Y Mab ydoed   a anydoed   dan y nodeu,
> A'e vam ar lawr   a'e bronn werthuawr wrth y eneu.

> To the house they went, no rampart, no door, wind-battered doorways; the Son, there he was, the one who was born under its shelter, mother on the ground with her precious breast held next to his lips.[15]

Stark insistence on the poverty of the birthplace again suggests the work of a Franciscan. But the allusion to the Virgin is no new thing. Devotion to the *lactatio* goes back to 'Blessed is the womb that bare thee, and the breasts which thou didst suck' of Luke 11:27. This theme recurs in poems by Bede, Hrabanus Maurus, Bernard of Cluny, and Peter the Venerable, as also the Psalter of pseudo-Bonaventure, which mentions the holy breast repeatedly.[16] So Madog's 'simplicity' uses ancient literary motifs.

Madog's innovating skill is more easily grasped when we turn back to our anonymous poem (tenth-century? twelfth-century?) on the Virgin and Child in the Red Book of Talgarth:

> Meckyt Meir mab yn y bru,
> Mat ganet y'r a'e kanvu,
> Llwybyr huan, llydan y deulu.

Meckyt Meir mab yn y chnes,
Mat ganet y'r a'e gweles,
Llwybyr huan, llydan y drachwres.

Meckyt Meir mab aduwyndawt,
Duw, penn perchen pob kiwdawt:
Y that, y neirthyat, y brawt.

Meckyt Meir mab ac urdyn y arnaw:
   Ny threis neb y deruyn.
Kein gyfreu, nyt ieu, nyt hyn.

Ny wyr ny bo kyuarwyd
Ual y deiryt Meir y gulwyd:
Y mab, y that, y harglwyd.

Gwnn ual y deiryt Meir, kyt bwyf daearawl prud,
   Y'r Drindawt ysprydawl:
Y mab a'e brawt knawdawl,
A'e that, arglwyd mat meidrawl.[17]

Mary fosters a child at her breast, fortunate his birth to those who found him, his course like the sun, his host wide-ranging. Mary fosters a child in her bosom, fortunate his birth to those who saw him, his course like the sun, his anger wide-ranging. Mary fosters a child of glory, God, chief possessor of every nation, her father, her strengthener, her brother. Mary fosters a child with authority upon him, none crosses his boundary; fair-spoken one, neither younger, nor older. The untutored do not know how Mary is of kin to God, her son, her father, her lord. I know, though I am but a shamefaced mortal, how Mary is kin to the spiritual Trinity, to her son and her brother in the flesh, and her father, the Lord who blesses and controls.

The lines are more archaic than those of Madog. They use the device of incremental repetition, found in the very earliest Welsh poetry of *c*.600. Though tenderness is not absent, the emphasis is on power and glory, as in *aduwyndawt* 'honour, nobility' (which the context shows cannot be 'gentleness').[18] The Red Book poem says nothing of the details of miserable squalor at Bethlehem (hay for a bed, rags for linen, and an icy draught of night air blowing in with no door to stop it) which Madog provides. Far from dwelling on the humility of the Incarnation, it speaks rather of how extensive is the Christ Child's host (his *teulu* or 'warband'), of his ineluctable anger, his legal possession of all nations, and his domain on which none trespasses; and, as regards the Virgin, on her power and status in having God as her kin. It well reflects a society where armed retinues, rights over communities, trespass, and the standing of one's kindred were no small matter. The phrase 'none crosses his boundary' is a striking expression of this. *Treisio*, here translated 'cross', has a basic meaning of 'vanquish, oppress, violate'. Trespass in the Middle Ages usually led to a brawl or worse, and attempts to sequestrate land were endemic; hence the poet's curious expression for the might of the Christ Child, that he is one on whose domain no man encroaches. This poem hence presents Virgin and Child as quasi-feudal figures, with rights expressed in terms of kinship and legal possession.

Against this, Madog presents a picture of a red-cheeked baby, helpless and poor, and now called *our* father and brother. The hymn *Dulcis Iesu memoria* (of English Cistercian origin, c.1200) had declared that, while the memory of Jesus was sweet, giving unalloyed joys to the heart, his actual presence was sweeter than honey and all things. Madog echoes this language, saying that it is honey to think of the infant Emmanuel, lofty and lowly. Finally, Madog glories in describing a Christ Child found in winter poverty, the Virgin sitting on the floor, her precious breast close to her baby's lips. The differences between the Red Book poem and Madog's poem mirror the revolutionary religious changes of the twelfth and thirteenth centuries.[19]

The Red Book poem reflects the stiff, hierarchical qualities of a Virgin and Child in Romanesque art, where Jesus, possessing symbols of power and wisdom, is enthroned on the knee of his mother. Though lacking neither beauty nor dignity, it contrasts easily with Madog's poem. Yet in one respect it does look forward to Madog, in the lines

Meckyt Meir mab yn y bru and *Meckyt Meir mab yn y chnes*. Here *bru* is translated 'breast, bosom' rather than 'womb', since what is unusual in this context is the verb *meckyt*. The verb *magu* means 'rear, nurture, nourish; to nurse, hold (a baby, etc.) in the arms'. Though apparently not used in the sense 'to suckle, give the breast to', it nevertheless indicates the intimate bond of mother and child. The context of fortunate birth and analogies in art suggest that the Child has been born, and is being presented to us by his mother for adoration.

Now, the representation in art of the Virgin suckling her Child was described by Southern as unknown in Western Europe before the twelfth century, where it appears in a Tree of Jesse in Dijon, Bibliothèque municipale, MS 641, produced at Cîteaux *c*.1110–20. The appeal by this Cistercian manuscript to the emotions is echoed in meditations on the Madonna and her baby by Eadmer and other disciples of St Anselm (1033–1109).[20] We can thus link this detail in the Red Book poem with the warmer devotion to the Virgin spread by Cistercians and others during the twelfth century; if so, a tenth- or eleventh-century date for the poem could be ruled out. It could perhaps be dated after 1140, when a colony from Clairvaux (daughter house of Cîteaux) reached Trefgarn, near Haverfordwest, moving in 1151 to Whitland, and leading to the foundation of further monasteries at Cwm-hir (1143), Ystrad-fflur (1164), Cymer (1176), and Aberconwy (1186). The Red Book verses could even be the work of a Cistercian at one of these houses in the wilder parts of *pura Wallia*, where they gained the confidence of the native Welsh as other monasteries in Wales, recruiting non-Welsh monks, did not.[21] Hence, perhaps, a Welsh poem due to their influence. Such a reference to the Virgin might also exclude a provenance in an older Welsh community like St Davids, which clung to older forms of devotion. In a poem discussed later in this book, Master John of Davids (*fl.* *c*.1148–*c*.1176) describes the Virgin as a rose amongst thorns, an epithet more reverent than novel, as it goes back to Caelius Sedulius in the fifth century. Even though intimate representations of Virgin and Child figuring amongst the relics of St Cuthbert (d. 687) and the Hiberno-Saxon Book of Kells (later eighth century) have been related to Coptic influences on Irish and Northumbrian Christianity, the expression *Meckyt Meir mab yn y bru* is more easily seen as reflecting not the old devotion of the seventh or eighth century, but the new one of the twelfth.[22]

When we return to Brother Madog, we find a second reference to the Virgin at the very end of his poem, which speaks of her power to assist mankind. Madog calls Christmas a blessed time when a son, 'each Pope's Sovereign', was born

| O Arglwydes | a wna yn lles, | a'n llud poenau, |
| Ac a'n gwna lle | yn tecca bre | yg gobrwyeu. |

Of a Lady who fashions our good, guards us from torments, and prepares our place in the fairest land as our recompense.[23]

The Virgin is able to help us, save us from damnation, and prepare a place in heaven for us. Her power in doing so reminds us of the Red Book poem. Yet there are fundamental distinctions between the two. The power of the Virgin in the first poem is entirely implicit. The poet does not ask for her help; she is quite passive; emphasis is rather on the might and glory of her son, brother, and father. The honour that the Virgin has come solely from her illustrious kinship. But in the closing lines of Madog's poem attention turns from the Christ Child to his mother, who here has an active and explicit role as our intercessor now and at the Last Judgement. Madog's poem can be compared in this with Irish evidence from the eighth century onwards. *Cantemus in omni die* 'Let us sing every day', the Latin hymn of by Cú Chuimne of Iona (d. 747) already mentioned, declares:

Amen, Amen, adiuramus
  merita puerperae,
Ut non possit flamma *pyrae*
  nos *dirae* decerpere.[24]

Amen, Amen, we invoke the merits of the mother, so that the
blaze of fearful hell may not be able to gather us in.

Other pleas to Mary come from Ireland. The anonymous
eleventh-century poem beginning *A Máire mín, maithingen*
'Gentle Mary, good maiden' provides a whole litany of
invocation to her:

Gentle Mary, good maiden, give us help, thou casket of the
Lord's body and shrine of all the mysteries. Queen of all who
reign, thou chaste holy maiden, pray for us that, through
thee, our wretched transgression be forgiven. Merciful forgiv-
ing one who hast the grace of the pure Spirit, join us in
entreating the just-judging king on behalf of his fair fragrant
children. O branch of Jesse's tree from the fair hazel-grove,
pray for me that I have forgiveness of my wrongful sin.

The poet goes on to address Mary as one who has 'saved
our race', asking her to pray to her Firstborn 'that he save
me at Judgement', calling her 'safeguard to glorious
Heaven' and so on.[25]
  How do these Celtic poems fit into the context of Christianity as a whole? In Eastern lands the cult of the Blessed
Virgin as advocate, helper, and mediatrix developed relatively early. Ephraem the Syrian (d. 373), Gregory of
Nazianzus (d. 389), John Chrysostom (d. 407), Cyril of
Alexandra (d. 444), and John of Damascus (d. c.750)
defended various aspects of it; but the West provides no
more than brief remarks of Irenaeus (d. c.202), Ambrose,
and Augustine. Only in the eighth century did a devotion
to the Virgin as 'door of heaven and hope of all Christians'
become widespread in the Latin Church, with the writings
of Ambrose of Autpert (d. 784) and Paul the Deacon (d.
799). These two had strong links with Benevento, near
Naples, and their Marian zeal may have been quickened

by Greek influences in southern Italy. In expounding their case for the Virgin as intercessor, Ambrose and Paul made possible the work of St Bernard of Clairvaux (d. 1153), who, above all, gave impetus to the cause of *Maria advocata nostra*.[26]

The Red Book poet does not here invoke the assistance of the Virgin; Madog does. Yet the texts from Ireland, Scotland, and the eastern Mediterranean show Madog was doing nothing new in asking the Virgin to help save men and women from hell and grant them a place in heaven. Even his vocative *Arglwyddes* 'Lady' indicates no innovation. The translation of the Antiphon *O mundi Domina* in the Exeter Book poem *Christ I* calls the Virgin 'lady by holy powers (*halgum meahtum*) of the glorious host and of this world', and the title *domina* had long been familiar in hymns and patristic sources.[27] T. S. Eliot's 'Lady, three white leopards sat under a juniper-tree' has early precedents.

Analysis of Marian elements in the Red Book poem on the Virgin and Child, and that by Madog on the Nativity, thus reveals a complex picture. The Red Book poem, perhaps of the later twelfth century, perhaps earlier, stresses the power and glory of the Child Jesus, and of the honour accruing to his mother through kinship with him. It does not mention God's humiliation in becoming man; on the contrary, it talks of Mary's elevation as *theotokos*, Mother of God. Although this last is a concept familiar to Latin and Greek Christianity alike, the working-out of its implications and stress on Mary's multiple kinship with God would have been readily understood in Celtic society. Emphasizing the Child, in no way invoking the Virgin's aid, its reference to her as nursing Jesus in her bosom may be an aspect of the twelfth-century humanizing, by Cistercians and others, of Marian devotion.

If the Red Book poem is perhaps of the twelfth century (even if an earlier dating cannot be ruled out), Madog's is almost certainly of the thirteenth. Though containing themes characteristic of that century, such as emphasis on the absolute poverty of the Holy Family, it tends rather to present traditional themes in a new way. Madog explores the wonder of the Incarnation, like Smaragdus before him and others since; but Madog also dwells on the weakness of the newborn baby, frail, tiny, and red-cheeked. Madog places the *lactatio* of Bede and Peter the Venerable not in a setting of glory, but in the context of a pauper mother and her baby. Even if his closing plea for the Virgin's intercession shows awareness of her power, it has implications different from those of the Red Book poem. There the Virgin is revered as one with power, the Mother of God; but in Madog's poem she is seen as a loving mother who cares for us.

After the Nativity, the Flight into Egypt. This is familiar to Celticists from the story of the Instantaneous Harvest, which makes an early appearance in Welsh and Irish poetry. The legend tells how on their journey the Holy Family pass a labourer ploughing a field, and the Virgin begs him to tell Herod's men the truth if they come that way. When Herod's men arrive soon after, the labourer tells them correctly that the fugitives passed while he was ploughing the field for sowing. But by now he is harvesting the crop, which has miraculously been sown, grown, and ripened, and the soldiers turn back in the belief that the Holy Family passed by months before. In some versions the ploughman is replaced by a sower, or the Christ Child speaks instead of the Virgin, but the outline of the tale remains the same.[28]

This story, well known to folklorists, has been reported in modern times from countries as far apart as Scotland, Romania, Portugal, and Russia. It has also been recorded in modern Aramaic of a Muslim holy woman fleeing an unwelcome marriage. Yet versions of the story in medieval literature are much rarer. Jackson refers to four only: an anonymous Welsh poem 'which presumably dates from the twelfth century'; an Irish poem of uncertain authorship which he dates to the thirteenth century; a fifteenth-century French miracle play; and some fifteenth-century Flemish carols. However, although the Welsh and Irish texts of the story have been considered as its oldest literary versions, it is argued below (a) that Jackson dates the Celtic texts too early, and (b) evidence suggests they derive from a source (of which Jackson was unaware) known from a thirteenth-century French poem. Jackson also mentions that representations of the theme 'are sometimes seen in medieval religious paintings'.[29]

What follows has thus been written with four objectives: to give a fresh survey of the material in the Celtic languages; to set out data for the tale from medieval England (which cast light on its history); to indicate the nature of Continental evidence for the legend, including material from art and literary texts unknown to Jackson; and to discuss whether, in the light of these, Jackson's views of the origin and diffusion of the story are still acceptable.

The Welsh version of the story forms the last part (lines 53–84) of a religious poem in the thirteenth-century Black Book of Carmarthen (Aberystwyth, National Library of Wales, MS Peniarth 1). The poem is usually dated to the twelfth century, from linguistic evidence rather than any doctrinal or narrative feature. This evidence consists of a detail of Old Welsh orthography presumed to be no later than about 1150, and the loanword *pilio* from Middle English *pilien, pillen*; but Jarman noted it would be risky to build much on this. The sole evidence for an early dating is the orthographical one, the spelling *per* for *peir* 'lord'; but this amounts to little, as the poem has many spelling blunders (such as *dwin* for *diwin, guenglad* for *guengulad, y win* for *y owin, hnni* for *hinni*).[30]

There is thus no convincing linguistic reason why the poem should not be dated closer to about 1250, the date of the Black Book itself. French poetry and art also provide grounds for dating the poem to the thirteenth century. It may be that the legend of the instantaneous harvest actually reached Wales from France. We shall return to this point below.

Ac eil guirth a wnaeth ehalaeth argluit
  a ergliw y voli.
Ban winnvis gochel y deli,
Sew fort y fföes iti
In yt oet aradur in eredic tir,
  herwit guir in gueini.
Y diwaud y Trindaud keli,
Ew a'e mam dinam, daun owri:
'A gur guin, turr guir gwydi ny a dav
  y geissaw in guesti,
Ar owris y owin iti
A gueleiste gureic a mab genti.
A diwed tithev ir olev guironet,
  ny'th omet in gweti,
In gueled in myned hebti,
Y randir a rad Duv erni.'
Ar hinni y doeth digiwoeth gwerin,
  llin Kaïn kadeithi,
Toriw anwar, enwir ev hinni,
Turr keisseid y keissav Keli.
Y diwod vn, gurthuun gurtharab,
  vrth y gvr a weli:
'A gueleiste dinion, din gowri,
In myned hebod heb drossi?'
'Gueleis ban llyuneis y lleutir deguch
  a weluch y medi.'
Sew a wnaethant plant Kaï,
Y vrth y medel ymchueli.
Druy eiroled Meir Mari, o'e gvybod,
  guybv Duv oheni.
Yt oet in y diffrid y gid a hi
Ysprid Glan a gleindid indi.[31]

And the generous Lord, who hears himself praised,
performed a second miracle. When he wished to avoid
capture, this is the way he fled, where a labourer was ploughing the land, working as was right. Christ of the Trinity said,
he and his immaculate mother, of excellent grace, 'Friend, a
band of men will come after us to look for our resting-place,
and ask you in haste, "Have seen a woman with a child?"
And tell the plain truth — our plea will not bind you — that
you saw us going past you, the field, and God's grace on it.'

At that there came a base rabble, descendants of wrathful Cain, a savage ill-natured mob, a crowd of pursuers hunting down the Lord. One, odious and churlish, said to the man he saw, 'Good fellow, have you seen anyone pass by you without turning aside?' 'I did when I harrowed the fair open land you see being reaped.' What the children of Cain did was to turn back from the reapers. Through the intercession of Mary, because she knew God, he remembered her; for the Holy Spirit and the purity that were within her were her protection.

This story, skilfully told, is a parable of moral innocence in a world of cruelty and deceit. It is strangely memorable, with the qualities of many great stories and myths. In asserting the power of the powerless it resembles the otherwise very different legend of Job's gold (also known in Middle Irish prose) a few lines before it, which tells how the destitute Job gave a suppliant all he had: the scabs on his skin, which yet miraculously turned to 'pure gold, wealth of the Trinity'.[32] One would like to know the identity of the poet (surely a cleric, and perhaps from Dyfed). Three points may in any case be made about his theological background. The epithet *dinam* 'immaculate' alludes to the then controversial question of the Virgin's Immaculate Conception, though unfortunately this helps little to date the poem. Eclipsed at the Conquest, the devotion reappeared in England after 1100; while Osbert of Clare (d. after 1139) at Westminster and Eadmer (d. 1141) at Canterbury defended it, by 1140 St Bernard of Clairvaux was opposing it, and about 1178 Peter of Celle was describing it as an islanders' fantasy (the water surrounding Britain had demented English brains). The devotion was later championed by Duns Scotus (d. 1308). In Wales, Einion Wann calls the Virgin *dinam* in his elegy for Llywelyn the Great (d. 1240).[33]

Second, the poet refers twice to Herod's man as 'children of Cain'. This is a medieval commonplace for evil men, and appears in the Red Book of Hergest, *Piers Plowman*, the *Towneley Plays*, and the writing of Robert Rypon (active at Durham before about 1400). Distantly related to the early Irish tradition that monsters, like Grendel in *Beowulf*, descended from Cain, it is minor evidence for the Welsh poet's learning.[34]

Much more important is his account of Job's gold, which sheds light on the poem's Continental links. Though this apocryphal tale was known in fifteenth-century France, Germany, and England, perhaps the earliest evidence for it is a sculpture (now in the Museum of Navarre, Pamplona) on a column capital of 1130–40 from Pamplona cathedral. It is thus possible that the Black Book poet took his reference to Job's gold from an oriental source reaching him via Spain and France. The last point is a crucial one. Jackson was sure the legend of the harvest derived from some early aprocryphal gospel text now lost, its initial dissemination being through religious written literature; that it appeared in early Welsh and Irish texts because Celtic Christianity had a taste for tales of the marvellous; and that it subsequently found its way into the folklore of the Continent of Europe and the Near East. Yet the sources for the legend of Job suggest a different model. There is no reason to regard the 'apocryphal tale of the marvellous' concerning Job as early, or to believe it had been preserved by Celtic Christians in isolation. At first sight the evidence would indicate that it was a recent arrival in Wales via the new pilgrim route between northern Europe and Santiago. The movement of legend across France in the opposite direction is, in fact, neatly proved by twelfth-century sculptures of Sigurd, the dragon Fáfnir, and the smith Regin at Sangüesa, twenty-five miles southeast of Pamplona. These derive from Norwegian and Swedish art, though they also have links with *Beowulf* and Norse saga, as well as pre-Norman sculpture in England and the Isle of Man.[35] The Sangüesa sculptures may have been commissioned by the Knights Hospitaller or Knights of St John, who had strong links with Scandinavia; if so, this would strengthen the case argued below that the Black Book poet owed his material to an international religious order, either the Augustinian canons at Carmarthen itself or one of the other orders established by the

Normans in south Wales. Against this, however, is important evidence produced by an Irish scholar from the
fifteenth-century Oxford, Bodleian Library, MS Rawlinson
B. 512. This contains a twelfth-century Irish prose text
describing how Job in his wretchedness was asked by a
leper for alms. Job gave him all he had, a 'hand's fill of
maggots and worms which were about his side', which
thereafter turns to 'gold ingots'. So the tradition was
known in early Ireland. Researchers are hence left with a
dilemma. Are our apocryphal legends early ones
preserved in a Celtic pool or backwater, when they had
disappeared in the rest of Europe (as Jackson thought)? Or
are our Welsh and Irish texts open to influences from over-
seas? Each case must be decided on its merits. The Welsh
legend of Job is closer to the Pamplona sculpture than it is
to the Irish text (Job's scabs, shown as disc-like objects on
the column capital, occur in the Welsh poem, and worms
do not appear). This would seem to suggest a Mediterranean origin for the story in the Welsh poem, and not an
Irish one.[36] If so, it would imply that the Welsh tales of Job
and the Instantaneous Harvest are not ancient Celtic
legends, but new arrivals from the Continent, presumably
coming via France.

Another Welsh instance for the legend of the harvest
occurs in a late poem, beginning *Y forwyn o fwy arail*, by
Hywel ap Dafydd ab Ieuan ap Rhys (*fl.* 1450–80), household bard to the Herbert earls of Pembroke at Raglan,
Monmouthshire. Sir Glanmor Williams described this as a
love-poem to the Virgin, 'describing the beauty of her
form and features', its author 'having doubtless been
deeply influenced by contemporary paintings of her'.[37]
Yet this is a slip. The poem does not describe the Virgin's
appearance but rather the Annunciation, Nativity,
Epiphany, and a few of Christ's miracles, adding some
apocryphal details to the Bible account. Williams was
thinking of Hywel's poem *Gwr wyf nid rhaid gwarafun*
(discussed later in this book), which his description fits
exactly. In the first poem, after describing Annunciation
and Nativity, Hywel states of the Virgin,

pan oyddyd hen vyd yw hyn
athalon gynt ythilyn
yr yd oedd yn yr edic
oy vlayn vry yn velyn yfric
yn yd ayddfed yw vedi
nyth welyd oedd yth ol di.[38]

When you were once long ago being pursued by your enemies, the corn that was being ploughed had, from its first-fruits upwards, ears of yellow; corn ripe for harvesting after you, and you were nowhere to be seen.

The legend also appears in the Irish bardic poem *Fuigheall beannacht brú Mhuire.*

Ga iarraidh ar muin Muire
do-rinne an mac míorbhuile,
an taobh fhíorbhán fa fhearta
'n-a míonghrán chaomh chruithneachta.

Innisidh is é gá ar
fear a faicsin tre achadh
an lásain tre lorg a mbonn
fásadh an colg 's an connall.

Tig an uairsin tres an ar
muintear Ioruaith [ga] n-adhradh
gér phrap soin do bás ga bhuain
ar bhfás an oir re haonuair

While being carried by Mary, her son being pursued performed a miracle; the white hill-side by his power changed into fine smooth wheat. A man says that he saw her going through the field while he was ploughing it, that from the earth trodden by their feet rises the wheat, awns and stalks. Herod's folk advance through the field closely following them [?]; though it was sudden, the corn was being cut after it had grown up immediately.[39]

The attribution and date of the poem pose problems. In the oldest manuscript, Dublin, Royal Irish Academy, MS

D ii 1, the 'Book of Uí Maine' (written about 1394 for Muircheartach Ó Ceallaigh, bishop of Clonfert in what is now County Galway), the poem is attributed to Gilla Bridi. This must refer either to Giolla Brighde Albanach ('Scotsman'), active about 1220, or to the Ulster poet Giolla Brighde Mac Con Midhe (c.1210–c.1272), born near Ardstraw, six miles south of Strabane. Of other attributions, those to fifteenth-century poets are clearly worthless, while that to Donnchadh Mór Ó Dálaigh (presumably the poet who died in 1244 rather than his namesake of about 1400) was described by McKenna as 'of little value'.[40]

The ascription of this poem to Giolla Brighde Mac Con Midhe has been called 'highly dubious'.[41] That to Giolla Brighde Albanach remains unproven (though worth investigation by those with access to his authentic poems). However, the uncertainty of scribes as to who wrote *Fuigheall beannacht brú Mhuire* suggests the identity of its author was unknown to them, and that we should hence treat the poem as anonymous. Yet, if it is anonymous, the case for dating it to the thirteenth century and not the fourteenth falls to the ground. The only sure *terminus ante quem* for its composition is that of the compilation of the Book of Uí Maine. We shall show below that the legend of the harvest was known before 1300 in England, France, Italy, and Sweden. Since we cannot prove that the Irish poem predates 1300, instead of containing an archaism, it may rather be further testimony for the diffusion of the legend throughout western Europe from northern France.

Nevertheless, the number of surviving manuscripts containing the poem, including the Book of the Dean of Lismore, implies its popularity in Ireland and Scotland during the fifteenth and sixteenth centuries. Poems by Tadhg Óg Ó hUiginn (d. 1448) must also refer to this legend, as no other tale of the Flight into Egypt alludes to an escape from pursuers. His source may have been the Irish poem cited above.

The Jews ever following her, 'twas no fit treatment for that queen! She had to flee as a deer into the desert while nursing God! Her tracker pursued her, yet, as the story goes, could not find her; God allowed her to be tracked, but a flood of his favour kept her safe.

He fled before Herod's folk; he and the Virgin had to flee afar; their miracles were their only resource.[42]

The story remained popular in Irish folklore into the twentieth century. Ó Caithnia, in listing various studies, notes one version from Kerry in which the corn is replaced by potatoes. He also mentions that in Irish the story is often linked with curses against pests damaging crops.[43]

How does the evidence from the Celtic countries compare with that from medieval England? This latter is scanty but widespread, suggesting that the legend was known in London, Oxford, York, and East Anglia. That the legend was familiar in thirteenth-century England is suggested by the Anagni Cope, of English origin (from a London workshop?), though it has long been in the cathedral treasury at Anagni, thirty-five miles east of Rome. It seems that the cope was donated to the cathedral about 1300 by Pope Boniface VIII, a native of the town. A panel on the cope shows two soldiers in chain mail interrogating the labourer as he stands by a field of ripe corn. Given the evidence for the legend in French literature and art, it is tempting to link the cope with the French culture of thirteenth-century England, even if the needlewomen were English.[44]

The miracle also appears on f. 14v of London, British Library, MS Add. 47682 (the 'Holkham Bible Picture Book' of 1325–35), and on some heavily restored fifteenth-century wall-paintings (mounted on linen) found some while ago in Norfolk, and dubiously linked with Bury St Edmunds Abbey. The story could also once be seen at Headington (now an Oxford suburb) in fourteenth-century wall-paintings discovered by Victorian restorers, who destroyed them, though fortunately not before a local antiquary had drawn copies.[45]

Besides examples from art, evidence occurs in English miracle plays. Rosemary Woolf pointed out that certain scenes in the Holkham Book can be related to medieval drama, so that, if this manuscript was produced in London, a play on the Instantaneous Harvest formed part of the London cycle, even though these plays have long been lost. However, as some evidence suggests an East Anglian provenance for the Holkham manuscript, the play cycle may actually have been from an East Anglian town with a Blackfriars community (the manuscript shows strong links with the Dominicans). There is also evidence that the legend was known (and performed?) in northern England from the York play of Christ's entry into Jerusalem (written perhaps before 1376, but rewritten in the earlier fifteenth century), where a character declares of Christ, 'He garte [made] corne growe withouten plogh, / Wher are [earlier] was none.'[46]

When we turn from Britain and Ireland to the rest of Europe, we find three literary instances of the story to add to the four cited by Jackson: in a thirteenth-century French poem in Paris, Bibliothèque nationale, MS fr. 1533; a prose version in a French incunable of twenty-nine folios, *De quelques miracles que l'Enfant Jésus fit en sa Jeunesse* (Lyon, n.d.), also in the Bibliothèque nationale; and in a Danish verse found with a fifteenth-century wall-painting of the miracle at Jetsmark, in the far north of Denmark.[47]

The Old French poem was edited by Reinsch in 1879. Although his edition has reached few British libraries, its importance as a thirteenth-century analogue of the Black Book poem is vital, and investigation of its dating, provenance, sources, and circulation would help Celticists to chart the early history of the present legend in more detail. The French poem tallies with the Black Book poem (but not the Irish one) in giving the Virgin a speech in which she addresses the labourer; the agreement between France and Wales, but not Wales and Ireland, weakens the argument that the legend spread from the Celtic countries rather than France. The passage following shows close parallels with the Black Book poem. Both give the speech of the Holy Family, the challenge of one of their pursuers, and the labourer's reply; both mention the labourer's plough; both emphasize the telling of the truth. In the Welsh poem Herod's man addresses the labourer as *din gowri*, where *gofri* means 'respectable, worthy'; in the French poem the seneschal or steward calls him *predons*, 'prudhomme, worthy man'. If the Welsh expression, which is not common, translates the French one, we could regard the French verses as the source of the Welsh poem. (Note: *enfes* = 'child'; *ocis* 'killed'; *trestot* 'completely'; *trespasser* 'pass by'; *forment* 'wheat'; *charue* 'plough'.)

La mere et son petit enfant,
Que ses enfes no soit ocis.
Il diront: Jes aure trais.
Sire prenne nos en ta pitie
Par la vostre sa.nte amistie.
Es vos le senechal venu
Trestot arme et fer vestu
En haut commença a crier
Et le predomes a apeler:
Predons, or ne me mentir mie,
Si chier come tu as ta vie,
Si tu veis par ci passer
.I. viel home ne trespasser
Et une fame et .I. enfant
Sor une mule chevauchant.
Et li predons li respondi:
Si m'ait diex, qu'i ne menti,
Ne par la foi, que je vos doi
N'a trestouz ceus de nostre loi,
Ainz puis que mon forment semai
Ne ma charue i atelai,
Dedenz mon champ mis por arer,
Ni vi ci home trespasser,
Ne puis se di, que je vin ça,
Fame a enfant n'i trespassa.[48]

Further light on the legend is shed by lists of the art historians, particulary that of Réau (who notes that the tale was later borrowed for hagiographical accounts of St Radegund of Poitiers).[49] The list below, of thirteenth-century works only, complements the literary evidence for the origins of the legend in northern France. A remark of Karen Gould is worth quoting here. Since the Instantaneous Harvest appears in art and literature in the thirteenth century only, its representation in a full-page miniature (f. 289v) in a manuscript of Yolande of Soissons 'reflects a knowledge of the most current traditions'.[50] This comment also suggests something of the fashionable background in England and Italy of the Anagni Cope.

It has not been possible to date exactly all the works mentioned below. Yet some of them may pre-date the Black Book poem. If so, this would tend to imply that the legend reached the Celtic countries from France and not vice versa. The following, therefore, shows the diffusion of the theme in thirteenth-century art:

A typanum at Rougemont, some 50 miles north-west of Dijon.

A wall-painting of before 1270, discovered in the 1950s, from the church at Asnières-sur-Vègre, about 16 miles west of Le Mans.[51]

A stained-glass window from Saint-Julien du Sault, situated some eighty miles south-east of Paris, between Sens and Auxerre.

An illustration in New York, Pierpont Morgan Library, MS 729, the Psalter and Hours of Yolande of Soissons, produced at Amiens in about 1275–85.

A wall-painting, of the last quarter of the thirteenth century, at Saint-Maurice-sur-Loire, to the west of Lyon.[52]

A panel in Châlons-sur-Marne cathedral.

A ceiling painting of *c*.1280 in the old church at Dädesjö, near the cathedral town of Växjö in central southern Sweden.[53]

A miniature showing three riders in chain mail, and a labourer showing them the way, in Cambridge, Trinity College, MS B.11.5 (244), a psalter from the priory of Augustinian nuns at Goring, Oxfordshire.[54]

Examples from art post-dating the year 1300 can be multiplied indefinitely.[55] Besides them may be mentioned one in a macaronic poem, sometimes called 'The Prisoner's Prayer', in London, British Library, MS Harley 2253 (famous for its anthology of English love-lyrics), which was written in the Ludlow area about 1340. The poem itself has been dated to the thirteenth century, though it may be slightly later (its first stanza was used by the Canterbury translator Michael of Northgate, writing about 1340). Its narrator pleads to the Virgin for his freedom, declaring *Of the sprong the ble, Ly souerein creatour*, 'Of you there sprang the harvest, sovereign creature', where the lack of any explanation suggests that by that date the miracle was well known in England.[56]

The above list of works of art, with the lyric from MS Harley 2253, has several functions. It shows that the belief of even recent art historians that the legend 'became a theme of art, especially in Netherlandish painting, during the fifteenth-sixteenth century, although only for a short period' is baseless. It also shows that the theme in art, appearing in glass, embroidery, and sculpture, as well as painting on wood, plaster, and vellum, is more extensive than Jackson's reference to 'medieval religious paintings' would suggest.

More important for literary scholars is the light it sheds on the origins of the tale. The American scholar T. P. Cross (1879–1951) described the story as an 'Irish myth'; Simon Evans of Lampeter thought the legend originated in the 'Celtic Church'.[57] Against this one can say that the Black Book account of Job's gold, an apocryphal story known in twelfth-century Navarre, points here to possible early links with the Continent. Further, the Black Book poem cannot be shown to be much older than the manuscript of about 1250 in which it occurs; while there is clear evidence for the theme in thirteenth-century French art and poetry. The Anagni Cope and Dädesjö roof-painting also prove the legend was known by 1300 in England, Sweden, and Italy. It is easier to reconcile this geographical distribution with a story diffusing from France rather than the Celtic countries, especially as nothing shows our Irish text must predate the fourteenth century.

If the immediate sources of the tale are French, how might it reach the Celtic countries? The most obvious answer is that it would have arrived in Wales first, via the religious Orders settling in Glamorgan and Dyfed after the Norman Conquest. These Orders were largely French-speaking. A thirteenth-century French poem (the work of Simon of Carmarthen) from the Augustinian priory of St John at Carmarthen, where the Black Book may have been written, still survives in an Oxford manuscript. Cowley thinks this poem a 'far cry from the ancient Welsh verses' which he thinks Welsh canons at the priory had copied into the Black Book.[58] But the precision of the Welsh poem's theological allusions, its delicate emphasis on the Virgin, and the very fact that it uses verse to tell a story, which is unusual in early Welsh (Irish bardic verse has a different tradition), may even suggest that its author was a cleric familiar with French verse. If so, it would not be a 'far cry' from Simon's poem (a near cry would be more like it). As noted, the Welsh poem resembles the French one in giving a speech to the Virgin, when the Irish one does not. If the legend began in France, reached Wales at an early date, and Ireland later and less directly, this would not be surprising.

Finally, is it possible to say anything about earlier forms of the legend? Jackson had a lucid account of the background he envisaged for such stories.

The mass of the more bizarre apocryphal lore which grew up in the early Church, and especially the Eastern Church, seems to have had a very special attraction for the Celtic monks, and whereas this material largely disappeared from the religious literature of Europe at an early period, it remained and flourished in the Celtic countries for centuries. Hence a considerable number of apocryphal legends which occur in Irish, and to some extent Welsh, literature are otherwise known almost exclusively in eastern sources like Coptic and Syriac texts, as well as in continental European folklore and representations in medieval art, but very little in regular European religious literature.

He then mentioned the Instantaneous Harvest amongst such themes, saying that there is little doubt that

[Its source] must have been some early Apocryphal Gospel now lost, and that its dissemination was in the first place through religious written literature; that it appears in early religious sources in Wales and Ireland because the Celtic Church was particularly fond of apocryphal tales of the marvellous; and that it eventually found its way into the folklore of the Near East and Europe.[59]

Jackson elsewhere expressed the same view in more direct form.

The Irish have always loved a good tale, and in the middle ages a good religious tale was irresistable to them, never mind whether it was considered uncanonical by the far-away church of Rome. Hence medieval Irish literature is full of fascinating stories, amounting sometimes to sheer folklore, which students of religious history on the Continent know only in very early Apocryphal sources or in the oldest practices of the primitive Church.[60]

Yet the evidence as regards the Instantaneous Harvest suggests another model. Nothing has been produced to show an ancient or Eastern origin for it; and, since its appearance in Welsh and Irish can be explained by influence from thirteenth-century France, there is no reason to assume it went through a process of being preserved for centuries by 'Celtic monks'. So there is a general lesson here, with applications beyond Celtic or Marian studies: to reject a model of history (especially one lending itself to romantic or exotic stereotypes) that does not tally with the facts, which should be as fully ascertained as they can be; a task now made easier for apocryphal texts in the Celtic languages by the research of recent decades.[61]

Notes

1. Henry Lewis, pp. 105–7.
2. Henry Lewis, p. xiv; *Dictionary of Welsh Biography*, pp. 607–8; Caerwyn Williams, 'Beirdd', 93, and his *Canu Crefyddol*, pp. 35, 39, n. 52; Greene, pp. xxxii–xxxiii; Oliver Davies, p. 176.
3. Cf. Murphy, pp. 26–9; Hirn, p. 261; Talbot, p. 118; Woolf, *English Religious Lyric*, pp. 144–5; Gray, *Themes*, pp. 22–3.
4. Glanmor Williams, p. 21.
5. *Dictionary*, pp. 607–8; Bennett and Smithers, p. 420; Dobson, pp. 293–9, 421; Ker, pp. 357–8; Breeze, *Medieval Welsh Literature*, pp. 53–5.
6. Bennett and Gray, pp. 367–8.
7. Gray, *Themes*, pp. 109–17, 263, n. 60.
8. Woolf, *English Religious Lyric*, p. 153; Gray, pp. 106–8, 262–3, and his *Selection*, p. 103–4.
9. Henry Lewis, p. 105; Clancy, *Earliest Welsh Poetry*, p. 163.
10. Gray, *Themes*, pp. 21–4.
11. Dreves and Blume, i, p. 40.
12. Breeze, 'Madog', 94.
13. Gray, *Selection*, pp. 7, 103–4.
14. Gray, *Themes*, pp. 107.
15. Henry Lewis, p. 106; Clancy, *Earliest Welsh Poetry*, p. 165.
16. Hirn, pp. 255–9, 384–7.
17. Haycock, pp. 117–18.
18. Rowland, p. 288.
19. Southern, *St Anselm*, pp. 233–4.
20. Ibid., pp. 238–40.
21. Glanmor Williams, pp. 19–20.
22. Mayr-Harting, pp. 189–90.
23. Henry Lewis, p. 107; Clancy, *Earliest Welsh Poetry*, p. 166.
24. Dreves and Blume, ii, p. 267; O'Dwyer, p. 56.

25. Murphy, pp. 45–51; O'Dwyer, pp. 67–8.
26. Obregón Barreda, pp. 189–99.
27. Burlin, pp. 140–1, 145.
28. Jackson, 'Note', 203, and 'Some Fresh Light', 203; Vendryes, 'Miracle', 64.
29. Jackson, *International Popular Tale*, pp. 120–2.
30. Haycock, pp. 122–5.
31. Haycock, pp. 127–9.
32. Haycock, pp. 121–2; Breeze, *Medieval Welsh Literature*, pp. 49–51.
33. Woolf, *English Religious Lyric*, pp. 116–17; Southern, *Medieval Humanism*, p. 146; D. Myrddin Lloyd, p. 25; Clayton, p. 87; Haycock, p. 135.
34. Lloyd-Jones, p. 360; Owst, p. 463; C. D. Wright, p. 8; Haycock, p. 135.
35. Breeze, 'Job's Gold', 275–8; Ó Macháin, 265–7.
36. Breeze, '*Beowulf*', 12–13.
37. Glanmor Williams, p. 483.
38. E. Stanton Roberts, p. 159.
39. Based on McKenna, *Aithdioghluim Dána*, i, p. 193; ii, p. 114, but with readings *a faicsin* and *gér* (both after Uí Maine) suggested by the editors of *Ériu*.
40. McKenna, *Aithdioghluim Dána*, p. xxxii; O'Dwyer, *Mary*, pp. 92–3.
41. N. J. A. Williams, pp. 10–11.
42. McKenna, *Dán Dé*, pp. xv, 71, 87.
43. Ó Caithnia, p. 142.
44. Christie, p. 101, plate LI.
45. Edwards, 'Medieval Wall-Paintings', 263.
46. Woolf, *English Mystery Plays*, pp. 390, 396.
47. Broby-Johansen, pp. 84–5; Schmidt, pp. 261–2; Mâle, p. 219; Kirschbaum, ii. cols 44–5.
48. Reiner, p. 64.
49. Réau, ii/2, p. 277.
50. Gould, p. 73.
51. Deschamps and Thibout, pp. 103–4, pl. 9.
52. Deschamps and Thibout, p. 143, pl. 75.
53. Anker, ii, p. 285, pl. 177.
54. Bennett, H. S., plate I; Ker, *Medieval Libraries*, p. 93; Breeze, 'Welsh *Cais*', 300.
55. Beissel, p. 624; Hirn, pp. 270, 389, n. 19; Kirschbaum, ii, cols 49–50; Schiller, i, p. 122; Brasas, pp. 24–5; Berger, *passim*; Edwards, 263–71; Bäumer and Scheffczyk, ii, p. 481.
56. Breeze, 'The Instantaneous Harvest and the Harley Lyric *Mayden Moder Milde*', 150.

57. Motif V211.1.8.3 in Thompson; Evans, p. 17.
58. Legge, pp. 68–9; Cowley, pp. 45, 152–3.
59. Jackson, *International Popular Tale*, pp. 119–22.
60. Jackson, *Celtic Miscellany*, p. 277.
61. Dumville, 'Biblical Apocrypha', 299; McNamara, pp. 1–13.

The Crucifixion

The Passion and death of Jesus, and Mary's role in it, were familiar enough to medieval people. In their churches they would see Christ's Cross in paint and wood, with Mary and St John the Evangelist shown standing beneath it. Yet this left a mark on Welsh and Irish poetry lighter than might be thought. Glanmor Williams commented with surprise on how few Welsh Marian poems mention the scriptural accounts of Mary, especially her place at Calvary.[1] McKenna similarly noted the somewhat peripheral and even theologically incorrect expressions of medieval and later Irish bards (especially that of a wrathful Christ on the Cross, seeking to destroy sinners, but being appeased or resisted by the Virgin).[2] It will be shown below that the best treatment by Welsh and Irish poets of Mary at the Cross can be found in descriptions of her tears and sorrows. Nevertheless, a certain poverty here as regards the central event of Christianity is curious. That it could not have been so is shown (somewhat unexpectedly) by a poem not usually associated with the Celts, *The Dream of the Rood*. This is of course written not in a Celtic language but Old English. Nevertheless, *The Dream of the Rood* has Celtic features which have never been properly understood. So, to provide a complete version of Mary's story, this chapter begins with *The Dream of the Rood*, an English poem which nevertheless has parallels in Irish learning, as argued below.

The Dream of the Rood is a dream-poem, in which a narrator tells how he slept and had a vision of the Cross, which tells him the story of Christ's death and resurrection, and of the part it played in those events. This remarkable poem, perhaps of the eighth or ninth century, survives in the Vercelli Book in north Italy and (a few lines) on a cross in an isolated church (national grid reference* NY 1068) near Ruthwell in south-west Scotland. At lines 90–4 of the Vercelli text the Cross makes a striking comparison of itself to the Blessed Virgin:

> Lo, the lord of glory, the guardian of the heavenly kingdom,
> Then honoured me over the hill trees,
> Just as he, almighty God,
> Honoured his mother also, Mary herself,
> Over all women for the sake of all mankind.[3]

Comment on how the Son of God honoured 'his mother also, Mary herself' (*his modor eac, Marian sylfe*) has been various. On the Cross exalted above other trees, Swanton cites *inter omnes arbor una nobilis* 'among all trees the only noble tree' from the hymn 'Pange lingua' by Venantius Fortunatus (d. 609?), and *Super omnia ligna cedrorum tu sola excelsior* from the York Breviary. He also mentions a link of Virgin and Cross in the second-century *Proof of the Apostolic Preaching* by St Irenaeus of Lyon.[4]

Huppé tried to relate the passage to *Paschale carmen* ii, pp. 30–9 by Caelius Sedulius (*c.*450), which says that as Christ cast off Adam's stain, so 'the blessed Mary springing from the root of Eve' atoned for Eve's sin. But Sedulius can hardly be a source for the English poem, since he does not mention the Cross, and the *Dream* does not mention Eve. Huppé's claim that *The Dream of the Rood* (lines 90–4) declares all women are honoured by the Virgin, and that the Virgin/tree parallel derives from play on *virgo, virga,* and *radix Jesse,* also fails to persuade.[5]

Papers on this point by Horgan and Ó Carragáin are discussed by Mary Clayton. She rejects Horgan's notion that the *Dream* here refers to the Virgin's Assumption, on the grounds that, while the Virgin ascended to heaven

*This is a location system for British Ordance Survey maps.

body and soul, the Cross remained on earth. But she accepts in part Ó Carragáin's linking of the *Dream* with the Assumption, because the poem echoes Gabriel's 'Blessed are you among women' (Luke 1:28), and because Crucifixion and Annunciation were both traditionally dated to 25 March. An implication unique in Old English literature has also been seen here: that, as the Cross began as a tree like any other, so the Virgin was also chosen arbitrarily, 'honoured for no special reason'.[6] Yet the suggestion shows a curious understanding of medieval Christianity, where the choice of Mary would be seen, not in modern terms as 'random' or 'accidental', but as part of God's pre-ordained plan, Mary having been chosen for her destiny before the foundation of the world to fulfil the prophecies of the Old Testament. More recently Ó Carragáin has emphasized again the parallels of Annunciation and Good Friday, as also between Mary and the Cross, each called upon to co-operate in the task of Salvation.[7]

Nevertheless, despite the above, *The Dream of the Rood* has never been properly related to patristic teaching on the Virgin and the Cross in the plan of Redemption. This is an early theme, distinct from those popular in the later Middle Ages of *Planctus Mariae* and the Virgin's Sorrows by the Cross (deriving from John 19:25–7, and familiar from the thirteenth-century 'Stabat mater dolorosa').[8] The idea of the Virgin and the Cross as agents in Mankind's salvation, contrasted with Eve and the Tree of Knowledge as agents in Mankind's fall, has a continuous history from the second century onwards. The theme of lines 90–4 of *The Dream of the Rood* is thus not as anomalous or aberrant as it seems. It can be related to a tradition going back to early Christian times.

The theme first appears in *Adversus haereses* (V.19) by St Irenaeus of Lyon (*c*.130–*c*.202). As a boy, Irenaeus knew St Polycarp of Smyrna (72?–157?), a disciple of St John the Evangelist, guardian of the Virgin Mary in her last years on earth. So the links of Irenaeus with the Blessed Virgin herself were not distant. Irenaeus says of Christ, 'if he has summed up, by his obedience on the tree, the disobedience perpetrated by means of the tree; if that deception of which Eve (a virgin espoused to a man) has been a miserable victim, has been dispelled by the good news of truth magnificently announced by the angel to Mary, also a virgin espoused to a man', then the bonds fastening mankind to death are now unloosed.[9] Irenaeus uses similar language in his *Proof of the Apostolic Preaching*, as Swanton notes:

> Adam had necessarily to be restored in Christ, that mortality be absorbed in immortality, and Eve in Mary, that a virgin, become the advocate of a virgin, should undo and destroy virginal disobedience by virginal obedience. And the sin that was wrought through the tree was undone by the obedience of the tree, obedience to God whereby the Son of Man was nailed to the tree.[10]

The Anglo-Saxons could hardly have read these passages for themselves. Irenaeus was almost unknown in the middle ages, and *Proof of the Apostolic Preaching* was thought lost until 1904, when an Armenian version turned up in Yerevan (capital of Armenia). But the work of Irenaeus circulated widely in early times, so that many later writers echo his association of Mary and the Cross in undoing the work of Eve and the Tree of Knowledge.

Some examples of this are curious. *De resurrectione*, by St Ephraem of Syria (306–73), declares of Christ, 'From on high he descended as a stream, and from Mary he came as a root; from a tree he came down as fruit, and as a first offering he rose again to heaven.' Severian of Gabala (d. *c.*408), in a sermon on the Cross, associates the Virgin with its mystery: 'Virginity is the root of the Cross, that is, the Virgin who bore him who suffered, giving birth not by the law of nature, but by the power and virtue of the Creator of nature.'[11]

More characteristic is a sermon preached on Christmas Day 386, where St Gregory of Nyssa (*c.*330–*c.*395) opposes Eve and Mary: 'that woman by means of a tree brought about sin; this woman by means of a tree restored good'. His contemporary St Ambrose (339–97), commenting on how

Jesus 'was led by the Spirit for forty days in the wilderness, tempted by the devil' (Luke 4:1–2), contrasts Adam with Christ, and goes on to contrast Eve with Mary, and the Tree of Knowledge with Christ's Cross: *per mulierem stultitia, per virginem sapientia, mors per arborem, vita per crucem.* Ambrose's commentary, used by Bede for his own commentary on Luke, was certainly known to the Anglo-Saxons.[12]

A variant of this theme occurs in sermon 45 by pseudo-Ambrose: *Eva nos damnari fecit per arboris pomum, Maria absolvit per arboris donum; quia et Christus in ligno pependit, ut fructus.*[13] This figures in such late manuscripts as Milan, Archivio Capella della Basilica, M35 (of the eleventh or twelfth century), and Salamanca, Biblioteca Universitaria, C.81 (fourteenth or fifteenth century), but also appears as an interpolation in a sermon of African provenance in Vatican City, Biblioteca Apostolica, MS lat. 5758, a seventh-century uncial codex from Bobbio. As Bobbio was an Irish foundation, maintaining close links with Ireland, it is possible that pseudo-Ambrose sermon 45 (of the sixth century or earlier) was known in the British Isles.[14]

In Eastern Christianity the theme is well attested. One instance appears in a Christmas sermon of before 359 attributed to Eusebius of Emesa (now Homs, Syria), surviving only in an Armenian translation. Declaring that Adam was created on a Friday and fell on a Friday, and that it was therefore necessary that Christ should suffer torment on that day and, at the sixth hour, taste the fruit of death, for Man to be victorious at the hour he met destruction, Eusebius continues,

> For the Tree in Paradise, lo, the Tree of the Cross. There is the woman, who brought sin into the world; here is the Virgin, who heard the words *Behold your mother.* Adam on that evil day stretched forth his hand; Jesus stretched out his fair and holy arms.[15]

The theme occurs again in the sermon *De coemeterio et de cruce* of St John Chrysostom (354–407), Bishop of Constantinople.

A virgin, a beam, and a death were the symbols of our defeat. The virgin was Eve; the beam, the Tree of Knowledge; the death, the punishment of Adam. But wait; a Virgin, a beam, and a death are also the symbols of victory. In the place of Eve is Mary; for the Tree of Knowledge of Good and Evil, the beam of the Cross; and for the death of Adam, the death of Christ. Do you see now how the Devil has been defeated by the very things with which before he triumphed?[16]

Chrysostom's works, often translated into Latin, were known in Anglo-Saxon England. His *De reparatione lapsi* and *De compunctione cordis* survive in a manuscript of English provenance, and Alcuin mentions his writings in the library at York.[17] Despite the fact that no Latin translation of the above text survives (though we have one in Armenian), Chrysostom's words show that the redeeming power of the Blessed Virgin and the Cross was a familiar theme in Greek Christianity. The identical passage appears in an Easter homily (also known in Bulgarian) probably by him, and in any case showing his influence.[18] A similar passage appears in a Christmas homily attributed to him:

Long ago the Devil deceived the virgin Eve, because of which Gabriel brought the good news to the Virgin Mary. Eve, having been deceived, brought forth a word that brings death; Mary, having heard the good news, conceived within her the Word which has obtained eternal life. Eve's words indicated the Tree which exiled Adam from Paradise; but the Word born of the Virgin revealed the Cross, which gave the Good Thief, representative of Adam, a place in Paradise.[19]

These passages thus reveal an unexpected link between *The Dream of the Rood* and Eastern Christianity in its widest sense, because the last sermon is known in Greek, Bulgarian, Armenian, Syriac, Georgian, and Arabic versions.

In Latin Christianity, a variant of the motif occurs in number 163 (on the Blessed Virgin's Nativity) of the second series of homilies written by Hrabanus Maurus (*c.*780–856) shortly before his death. This declares,

> Per quatuor fuit perditio mundi: per mulierem, per virum,
> per lignum, per serpentem; per quatuor restauratur: per
> Mariam, per Christum, per crucem, per Joseph.

> The loss of the world came about because of four things: a
> woman, a man, a tree, a snake. But by four things it is
> redeemed: by Mary, by Christ, by the Cross, by Joseph.

These sermons had almost no influence. Homily 163, original in expression and using varied sources, is known only
from an edition published at Cologne in 1617.[20] Yet it
provides evidence for knowledge of our theme in Anglo-
German circles, since Hrabanus was a pupil of Alcuin of
York.

Further light on this point comes from slightly earlier
Irish sources. In the Marian hymn 'Cantemus in omni die',
Cú Chuimne of Iona (d. 747) declares 'By a woman and a
tree the world first perished; by the virtue of a woman it
returned to salvation.'

> Per mulierem et lignum
>   mundus prius periit;
> Per mulieris virtutem
>   ad salutem rediit.[21]

The reference to *mulier* and *lignum* proves a link with the
theme as expressed by Hrabanus. Though it does not actually mention the Cross as second *lignum*, the poem (dated to
between 693 and 704, and probably earlier than later)
suggests the present motif was known in Irish circles at the
time the Ruthwell Cross was carved.[22] Irish influence did
not cease in Northumbria after the Synod of Whitby; and,
since Professor Stanley now thinks *The Dream of the Rood* is
the work of one man, if the English poem were written about
700, lines 92–4 of it would parallel those in Cú Chuimne's
hymn; even if the actual Ruthwell Cross inscription may be
as late as the ninth century.[23] If *The Dream of the Rood* were
old as the year 700, then the association of the Blessed Virgin
and the Cross in Man's Redemption would be a theme familiar both in Iona and in early Christian Northumbria.

The evidence set out above shows how texts, ranging from as far apart as Scotland and Syria, bring together the Blessed Virgin and the Cross in the plan of Redemption. Because such an association can be revealed as something known throughout Christendom from very early times, we can see *The Deam of the Rood* here as part of a great tradition. At the same time, the patristic texts indicate the originality of the Old English poet. He refers, not to Eve and the Tree of Knowledge, but to the Cross as honoured among other trees as Mary was blessed among women, echoing the words of Gabriel and of Elizabeth at Luke 1:28, 42. If it was he who first united those scriptural sources with the patristic tradition of Virgin and Cross in Man's Redemption (implicit, as we have seen, in the Marian hymn by Cú Chuimne of Iona), it would be a further tribute to his genius.

The tradition linking the Virgin and the Cross is patristic, ancient, learned, and intellectual. That of her tears of blood is almost its opposite: late, popular, legendary, and emotional. Put together, the two themes show the varying motifs available to writers in the Celtic lands on the Virgin and the Crucifixion, though few of them can be more striking than that of the tears of blood wept by Mary as she watched Christ being crucified. First recorded during the thirteenth century in Latin, German, and English poetry, the tradition was clearly known in the fifteenth century to Welsh and Irish bards, as well as to the author of the play on Cain and Abel in the Cornish *Ordinalia*. However, despite its popularity in medieval Britain, the story in our time survives within the British Isles only in the Irish *Gaeltacht*. In Britain itself it apparently died out with the Reformation.

Yet the popularity of this tradition in medieval Britain and Ireland has passed unnoticed by modern scholars of Welsh and Cornish, who have misunderstood the passages where its influence appears. Celticists have also failed to appreciate that, since the legend appears in Ireland, Wales, and Cornwall as a result of English and Continental influence, it owes nothing to the secular tears of blood mentioned in early Irish literature. The conclusion suggested by the evidence presented below is thus somewhat paradoxical: that the Virgin's tears of blood of modern Irish folklore, far from being 'native' or 'Celtic', are actually a relic of an international European tradition that was particularly well developed in England.

The earliest source mentioning the Virgin's tears of blood appears to be the text *Vita Beatae Mariae Virginis et Salvatoris rhythmica,* allegedly written by a German-speaker living in Istria or Friuli about 1200. In it we hear how the Virgin 'weeps tears of blood and finally lies in a dead faint across her son's body'. Aided no doubt by such religious sensationalism, the poem had enormous influence on German vernacular poetry, including the lives of the Virgin by Walther von Rheinau, Brother Wernher, and Brother Philip the Carthusian, as well as the *Grazer Marienleben.*[24]

However, whether the tradition of the Virgin's tears of blood actually begins with the *Vita Beatae Mariae* rather than elsewhere in Europe is more difficult to say. It may have done, since the weeping of bloody tears was already a topos in German. The aged Charlemagne shows his grief by weeping blood in *Rolandslied,* the Middle High German translation (made about 1170) of the *Chanson de Roland.* So tears of blood were a recognized literary motif amongst speakers of German. The question also arises as to whether the tears of blood appear in England through German influence and, if so, in what way. Although we can point to at least one copy of *Vita Beatae Mariae* in England, at Canterbury (where it belonged to a monk at Christ Church), we are here perhaps on safer ground in talking of oral transmission, as in modern Ireland, where this text also circulated.[25]

The earliest English sources mentioning the Virgin's tears of blood date from the thirteenth century. One of the first of them is a dialogue of the Virgin with Christ crucified, found in several thirteenth- and fourteenth-century manuscripts, in which Christ tells his mother to have pity on her child, and to wash away her bloody tears, which grieve him more than his death.

Moder, reu upon thi beren!
Thou wasse awey tho blodi teren;
It doth me werse than mi ded.[26]

The same theme occurs in another lyric on the Passion,
perhaps in Worcestershire dialect, in Cambridge, Trinity
College, MS 323 (possibly of Franciscan provenance). The
themes of the poem are remarkable for their violence: we
are told that the Virgin thought she would go mad, that
her heart began to bleed, that she wept tears of blood.

Hire thucte a miste aweden,
Hire herte bigon to bleden,
Teres hoe wep of blod.[27]

Another thirteenth-century example of the tears comes
from a springtime lyric on the Passion, 'Somer is come and
winter gon', of the mid-century or later:

Mayde and moder thar astod,
Marie ful of grace,
And of here eyen heo let blod
Uallen in the place,
The trace ran of here blod.[28]

Later examples are as common. In his prayer to Christ, a
knight says:

For loue thou tholedest [didst suffer] woundes depe,
Thin hondes therled [pierced], and eke thi fete;
Thy moder blodi teres lete ... [29]

This may be paralleled from many other fourteenth-
century English poems, including 'The Charter of Christ',
of which charter the Virgin is described as witness:

And namely my moder swete;
That for me blody terys gan lete;

dialogues of the Virgin and St Bernard:

> The blod out of hire eghen ron
> Almost hire herte clef atwo ... ;

> That sorow so to hir hert thrang
> That blude ran of hir eghen bright;

and *The Northern Passion*, where Christ commits his mother to the care of St John:

> Oure ladi herde tho wordis swete
> Teris of blod sche gan doun lete
> Al was hire face hid in blod
> Ther sche beheld ihesu on the rod.[30]

By a curious chance, the first of these four Middle English texts was actually translated into Irish. Yet, as this was apparently done at some date between 1461 and 1463, it could not have influenced the Irish poems discussed below, some of which long predate that.[31]

Of special interest amongst these examples, in the light of native Irish poetry, is one in London, British Library, MS Harley 913, a volume of Middle English lyrics compiled about 1330 in Ireland, well known as one of the earliest examples of Anglo-Irish literature. It speaks of the Virgin's shedding four tears of blood. The detail seems otherwise unknown in English, but is paralleled in Irish.

> For to wep ho nad no mo
> Than .IIII. bitter teris of blode.[32]

In this context we may note a translation, also in MS Harley 913, of the meditation *Respice in faciem Christi tui*, beginning,

> Loke to thi louerd, man, thar hanget he a rode,
> And wep hyf tho mist terres al of blode.

The reference must reflect the cult of the Virgin's tears of blood, suggesting how familiar it was in the Irish Pale. The poem occurs as well in Cambridge, St John's College, MS 15, which may likewise have had Irish connections, as it belonged to Robert of Portland, who describes himself in it as bishop-elect of Dromore, and who in 1428 was provided to Emly.[33]

The theme of the Virgin's tears of blood remained popular in fifteenth-century English, whether in an appeal by the Virgin in a manuscript from Muchelney, Somerset,

Se my blody terys fro my herte roote rebowne;

a Scottish account of the Passion and the Virgin's part in it;

Scharp bludy teris hir cristell eyne out ran;

or a ballad-like lyric on the hours of the Cross,

Hys mother wepte water and blode
　Standyng here dere sone by;
I can not tell wheder of them
　More rufull was to see.[34]

One late poem from northern England describes a *pietà* on which the Virgin's tears have been painted, thereby offering proof for this theme in art. It is worth pointing out that this detail on statues, carvings, images, and book illustrations (especially in Books of Hours) would be important in disseminating knowledge of this motif; that we easily forget this, as the detail would often be lost even if the work itself escaped the wrath of the reformer; and that at least one of the Irish passages below can be related to the tradition of the *pietà*.

Purtryed and peyntid piteously,
This ymage was with terys of blode,
As for a meroure veryly
Of oure lady I understode.
Hir sone uppon hir kne did ly,
All rent and revyn brought fro the rode.[35]

So pervasive was the theme that it appears even in carols, including the following bittersweet example from the fifteenth century.

> Oure dere Lady she stood him by —
> M and A, R and I —
> And weep water ful bitterly
>   And teres of blood ever among

— that is, the Virgin wept continuously as she stood by the Cross.[36]

The emphasis on the Virgin's weeping water and blood also appears in carols to the Virgin by the minor Franciscan poet James Ryman, who was active towards the end of the fifteenth century, and whose work provides us with a final English example of this theme.

> As Moyses yedre, that was so goode,
> Turned the waters into bloode,
> So did Mary moost myelde of moode
> Under the cros, whereas she stoode
>   Ful sore weping:
> Her teres ran with blode bleding.[37]

The above examples have been quoted at some length to emphasize how popular this theme was in medieval English poetry, how it appears consistently there from the thirteenth century up to the eve of the Reformation, and how it figures even in the English poetry of Scotland and Ireland. Even without the evidence of iconography or non-literary texts, the above suggests that a belief in the Virgin's tears of blood was cherished wherever English was spoken. Tears were a particular cult of the latter Middle Ages.[38] Hence, no doubt, the absence of material before the thirteenth century.

How does the above compare with what we find in literature in the Celtic languages? The most detailed study related to this is by Vernam Hull.[39] He certainly proves that, in Irish literature, tears of blood other than those of the Virgin Mary were known from early times. To his examples may be added others, one being of special interest. It occurs in the eighth-century religious poems of Blathmac, who writes of the witnesses at Calvary that it would be no wonder if there were 'a heavy tear of blood, a drop of blood, upon every cheek keening the captive'. But it is significant that Blathmac does not attribute the tears to the Virgin personally, and in fact places remarkably little emphasis on her grief.[40]

Despite the fact that Hull shows non-Marian tears to be well attested in Irish, he assumes that tears of blood in the other Celtic languages must be an inheritance from the days of Celtic unity. Nor does he make any reference whatever to the Virgin's tears of blood, either in English or any other language. The approach to the Welsh, Cornish, and Irish material in what follows thus differs considerably from that suggested by Hull.

The only Welsh instance of tears of blood quoted by Hull is one, unfortunately somewhat unclear, from *Canu Heledd*.[41] But there are at least six more which are quite unambiguous. What seem to be the earliest come from two poems written about 1460 by Ieuan Deulwyn and Dafydd Epynt. In an elegy for two Powys men, Dafydd Fychan of Llanbister and Ieuan ap Llywelyn of Llangurig, who were murdered when travelling through the mountains of mid-Wales, Ieuan compares himself to the Virgin at Calvary.

Yma 'ddwyf am y ddeufab,
Mal Mari am welïau 'i mab:
Gwaed oedd o'i llygaid iddi,
A gwaed ail o'm llygaid i.[42]

Here am I for the two sons, like Mary for the wounds of her son, with blood flowing from her eyes, and blood flowing from mine.

The reference from the Brecknock poet Dafydd Epynt comes in his unpublished praise-poem to the Virgin, *Mair Forwyn mae ar foroedd*. Dafydd describes the crucified

Christ entrusting his grief-stricken mother to the care of St John:

> Gwaed o'r iad a gydredodd
> A gwaed y wraig gwedy rodd;
> Wedi'r corff roi i waed er caith
> Gwaed ai'n olwg dyn eilwaith.[43]

After bestowal, the woman's blood and blood from his brow streamed down together; after his body gave its blood for slaves, blood flowed again in the eye of the woman.

A third reference to the Virgin's tears of blood occurs in an elegy by Gutun Owain (fl. 1450–98) for Alswn Vechan, of Bersham, two miles west of Wrexham:

> Gallwn wylaw, heb gellwair,
> Gyda'i mam, ddagreu gwaed Mair.[44]

Without jest, I could weep with her mother the Virgin's tears of blood.

A fourth comes at the opening of an elegy for Siôn ap Madog Pilstwn, or Puleston (Alswn's husband), by Guto's Glyn (*c.*1435–*c.*1493):

> Wylofus wyf fal afon,
> Wylais waed ar wely Siôn.[45]

I am as full of tears as a river, I wept blood on Siôn's bed.

This fourth reference occurs specifically in the context of the Virgin and the Cross, since Guto goes on to speak of the gold which people placed on them to intercede for Siôn when he was ill. It seems, as Dafydd Bowen points out in his notes, that Guto refers to an actual image of the Virgin and the Cross at Bersham. This Bersham Virgin may well have been shown weeping tears of blood.

The Virgin's tears of blood are also mentioned in an elegy by Dafydd Llwyd (*c.*1420–*c.*1500) of Mathafarn, near

Machynlleth, for a young girl killed by bubonic plague (as
we know from his description of her symptoms). With the
grief he feels now, he declares, the earth itself would
weep; he knows a stone once cried out under such duress;

A Mair gynt yn ei mawr gur,
Gwaed a wylodd, gyd-dolur.[46]

And Mary once in her great affliction wept blood in like
sorrow.

The last of these examples comes from an anonymous
poem of the late fifteenth century to the shrine of Our
Lady of the Throne at Llanystumdwy, near Criceth in
Gwynedd. The Virgin speaks imploringly to the crucified
Christ,

Ag a wylawdd o'i galyn
Dagrau gwaed er y grog wynn.[47]

And, from entreating him, she wept tears of blood for the
holy Cross.

That the Virgin's tears of blood must have been equally
familiar in Cornwall is proved by the words, quoted by
Hull, in which Eve expresses her feelings of grief after the
murder of Abel in the Cornish *Ordinalia*:

Yma ken th'm the ole
Daggrow gois in gvyr hep mar.[48]

Truly there is reason for me to weep tears of blood, without
doubt.

The full significance of these words was not understood
until recently, and becomes clear only in the context of the
Virgin's tears of blood. Because in Christian typology the
death of Abel prefigures that of Christ, the unknown
author of the Cornish play showed the first Eve weeping
tears of blood at the death of her son, Abel, as he must

have believed the second Eve wept wept tears of blood at the death of her son, Christ. The making of such a parallel would be a typically medieval approach to the Bible, not least in drama. This feature here is a tribute to the subtlety of the unknown author of the play, and perhaps even more so to that of his audience, if they could be expected to appreciate it. It underlines the way in which medieval religious drama is full of patterns, being part of a single, overarching narrative.[49]

No reference in Irish to the Virgin's tears of blood predates the fifteenth century. What may be the earliest comes from a poem in praise of the Virgin by the Connacht bard Tadhg in Óg and Ó hUiginn (d. 1448), which repeats the motif of the numbered tears occurring in MS Harley 913. In Irish the tears are reduced from four to three:

> An leanbh ré luigheadh an ógh
>   A fhearg níor cuireadh ar gcúl
> nó gur dheonuigh Rí na ríogh
>   síodh ar a trí deoruibh dhún.

The child, the Virgin's spouse, did not put his anger aside until he granted our pardon at her three tears.[50]

Tadhg mentions this belief in another poem.

> Trom ré n-íoc gion go mb'eadh leis
> na trí déara do dháilis
>   it luighe a Mhoire ar do Mhac
>   is dá Mhuire oile iomad.

Most precious did he consider the three tears you shed when fainting over your son, with the other two Maries at your side.[51]

The second instance is of interest in giving a hint of the *pietà* in fifteenth-century Irish poetry, at a time when this was a fairly common motif in English and Continental art and poetry.

In these examples the three tears are not said to be

bloody, as the four tears are in English. But in two anonymous bardic poems of this period the reference to the Virgin's tears of blood is made clear:

> Ag labhairt re a dalta dhí
> uisge a dearc do dhoirt Muire:
> geall caithmhe ar fhuil an abhra
> do chuir d'aithle a hagallmha.[52]

Mary wept while speaking with her foster-son [St John]; she wept more blood [than water] after her conversation.

> Do cheannaigh — fa cunnradh sochair —
> síoth a dalta ar a deoir ndeirg.[53]

With her red tear – blessed bargain – Mary bought her son's appeasement.

The same theme appears in a poem by the Observant friar, Philip Bocht ('the poor') Ó hUiginn, who died in 1487, but of whose biography little is otherwise known.

> A sgarthain an uair do b'ál
> ris an uaidh do athraigh seol
> ar a leanb do luigh an ógh
> nír mhór nar fhuil dearg a deor.

When they would lead her away from the grave, she turned and cast herself on his body: almost as blood was the red of her tears.[54]

In laments of the Virgin collected from modern speakers of Irish, the tears of blood shed by Mary for her son are still a common motif.[55]

What relationship do the Celtic tears of blood attributed to the Virgin bear to those in English and Continental sources? It is argued here, first, that the Virgin's tears in Welsh, and Eve's in Cornish, derive from English influence. The evidence in England for the Virgin's tears of blood is strong: evidence in Wales and Cornwall for tears of blood not the Virgin's is weak. Second, the Irish bards also surely received the theme from outside, that is, in their case, from beyond the Irish-speaking part of Ireland. So much is suggested by the fact that the theme appears in Hiberno-English a century before it appears in Irish; that the use of the theme in Irish displays details closely paralleled in English and Continental sources; and that it occurs in Irish bardic poetry with other themes certainly of English or Continental origin. Moreover, if this theme did not enter Irish from beyond Gaelic Ireland, why does it not appear until as late as the fifteenth century, when non-Marian tears of blood appear in other Irish religious poetry as early as Blathmac?

Finally, is it possible to suggest exactly how the theme might have reached the poets who used it, especially those in Ireland who were furthest from other Continental influences? What we know of fifteenth-century Irish literature provides some clues on this. First, the Irish instances of the Virgin's tears given here are more varied than those in English. All the English instances, except that in the northern poem on the *pietà*, describe the Virgin as standing by the Cross, and weeping blood in grief for her son. But two of the Irish poems speak of these tears as assuaging Christ's anger, while another describes the Virgin as throwing herself onto Christ's body when about to be led away from his grave. (The last also contains the phrase *nír mhór nar fhuil dearg a deor*, which Brian Ó Cuív thought might be taken 'her tears were almost as red blood'.) There is nothing at all like this in English. The differences shown by the use of this theme in Irish suggest it entered Irish tradition in a variety of ways. The detail of tears appeasing Christ's anger might result from a process of oral transmission; that of the Virgin's throwing herself on Christ's body is close to that in a written source, the *Vita Beatae Mariae*; while Tadhg Óg's description of the Virgin's fainting over her son with the two Maries at her side may show the influence of a *pietà*. This last would imply an influence entering Ireland during the fifteenth century, since (as Rosemary Woolf pointed out) the *pietà* is unknown anywhere before that date.

In the diversity of the ways in which it apparently reached the bards, the theme of the Virgin's tears of blood can be compared with that of the Charter of Christ. This is a devotional motif, surely of Middle English origin, which appears in other poems by Tadhg Óg Ó hUiginn and Philip Bocht Ó hUiginn, as well as in a translation of an English poem on the subject by Philip's contemporary, Uilliam Mac an Leagha. In all this the Charter exactly resembles the Virgin's tears. Yet the use of it by Tadhg Óg and Philip Bocht not only lacks the relentless elaboration of the English texts, but also contains features without parallel in English (as when they describe the Cross as the Charter, and not Christ). The implication is that these two bards used an oral tradition which had changed or become distorted in transmission. Uilliam Mac an Leagha, on the other hands, who had a written text before him, has left a translation remarkable for its accuracy. He includes all the features of the Charter, including the reference to 'my moder swete, / That for me blody terys gan lete' quoted above: *in ógh mhilis bhúidh charthanach do shíl déra fola.*[56]

If we had to point to one particular movement by which these and other aspects of a wider spiritual life came to fifteenth-century Ireland, it would be that of the new Observant amd Third Order Franciscan communities, whose oral and written influence comes as a second spring (or Indian summer?) in medieval Irish literature and devotion. It was, for example, apparently through the Third Order Regular house at Rosserk in north County Mayo, not so far to the west of Ó hUiginn territory, that the text of the pseudo-Bonaventuran *Meditationes Vitae Christi* was brought to Connacht, where it was soon translated into Irish by a canon of Killala Cathedral. This translation contains an interpolation on the number of Christ's wounds which finds its parallels, not in the English literature of this period, but in the revelations experienced by St Frances of Rome (1384–1440).[57] This Italian tradition then found its way, via the Irish translation of the *Meditationes*, into the Irish translation of the Middle English poem on the Charter of Christ quoted above. The diverse histories of the themes of the Charter and Wounds (both also found in Welsh) we are fortunate to know in some detail, and they certainly suggest the complex international patterns to be found in the late medieval poetry of the Celtic lands. It would not be strange if it was by similar routes, perhaps including those available to the new Franciscan orders, that the international theme of the Virgin's tears of blood reached Gaelic Ireland. If so, it will attest the devotion in those parts both to Christ crucified and to Mary at Calvary, who was remembered and invoked at that place: *Recordare, Virgo Mater Dei, dum steteris in conspectu Domini, ut loquaris pro nobis bona*, 'Be mindful, Virgin Mother of God, of when you stood in the sight of the Lord, that for us you should speak well.'

Notes

1. Glanmor Williams, p. 482.
2. McKenna, *Dánta*, p. ix.
3. Clayton, p. 206, n. 103.
4. Swanton, pp. 128–9.
5. Huppé, p. 101–2.
6. Clayton, pp. 206–7.
7. Ó Carragáin, 'Rome Pilgrimage', pp. 630–1.
8. Gray, *Selection*, p. 111.
9. Casagrande, p. 49.
10. Ibid., pp. 50–1.
11. Cignelli, pp. 95–6.
12. Mayr-Harting, pp. 210–11.
13. Casagrande, p. 378.
14. Barré, 'Le "mystère"', 92, 94–5; Lowe, p. 309.
15. Casagrande, p. 96.
16. Migne, xlix, col. 396.
17. Farmer, p. 94.
18. Migne, lii, col. 768; cf. de Aldama, pp. 53–4.
19. Migne, lvi, cols 392–3; Cignelli, p. 96.
20. Barré, 'La nouvelle Ève', 21, and his *Les homéliaires*, pp. 13–17; Longère, pp. 41–2.
21. Dreves and Blume, ii, p. 266.

22. Murphy, p. 22; cf. Anderson, p. 16, n. 68; Byrne, pp. 247, 257.
23. Stanley, pp. 384–99; Breeze, 'Date', 3–5.
24. Graef, i, p. 261.
25. Lipphardt, pp. 403, 432; Wesle, pp. 267, 268; McNamara, *Apocrypha*, pp. 123–5.
26. Gray, *Selection*, p. 19.
27. Silverstein, p. 16.
28. Ibid., p. 28.
29. Brown, *Religious Lyrics of the XIVth Century*, p. 224.
30. Horstmann and Furnivall, *Minor Poems*, ii, p. 650, i, p. 301; Horstman, ii, p. 275; Foster, p. 204.
31. Mac Niocaill, 216; Breeze, 'Charter', 119.
32. Heusler, p. 111; cf. Ó Caithnia, p. 156; Bliss, p. 723.
33. Brown, *Religious Lyrics of the XIVth Century*, p. 2; cf. Bliss, p. 726.
34. Brown, *Religious Lyrics of the XVth Century*, pp. 16, 132, 138.
35. Woolf, *English Religious Lyric*, p. 258.
36. Sisam and Sisam, p. 479.
37. Greene, p. 133, and cf. p. 397.
38. Adnès, col. 299.
39. Hull, pp. 226–36.
40. Carney, p. 45; O'Sullivan and Ó Riain, p. 76.
41. Ifor Williams, *Canu Llywarch Hen*, p. 40; Rowland, pp. 437, 488, 597.
42. Cynddelw, p. 153; cf. Ifor Williams, *Casgliad*, pp. 97–8, and Glanmor Williams, p. 482, n. 8.
43. Breeze, 'Virgin's Tears', 116.
44. Bachellery, p. 243.
45. Bowen, p. 45; cf. Clancy, *Medieval Welsh Lyrics*, p. 215.
46. Harries, p. 128; cf. G. P. Jones, p. 123.
47. G. Hartwell Jones, p. 338; cf. Glanmor Williams, p. 482, n. 8.
48. Cf. Harris, p. 19.
49. Murdoch, p. 52.
50. McKenna, *Dán Dé*, pp. 2, 70, and cf. pp. xvi, 3, 20, 71, 87.
51. McKenna, *Dán Dé*, pp. 11, 79, and cf. Ó Caithnia, p. 155.
52. McKenna, *Dioghluim Dána*, p. 85.
53. Ibid., p. 91.
54. McKenna, *Philip Bocht Ó hUiginn*, pp. 62, 167, and cf. pp. xvii, 18, 112, 139, 194.
55. Partridge, pp. 21, 45–6, 52, 79–80, 98, 204, 239, 290, 291.
56. Mac Niocaill, 204–21; cf. Poppe, p. 98.
57. Breeze, 'Number', 84–91, and 'Postscripta', 50–1.

The Assumption and the Last Judgement

With the Assumption comes the end of Mary's earthly life; with the Last Judgement comes the end of time. Both subjects provided matter for Welsh and Irish poets, and both included surprises. The first is thus linked to the legend of Mary's girdle, thrown down as she ascended to heaven; the second to that of her rosary, placed in the scale of judgement to tilt it in the favour of mortals. So these traditions indicate the power of relics and of the rosary for medieval people; as also their fear of wrath to come.

We begin with the Assumption, the belief that the Virgin Mary's body did not suffer corruption, like those of mortals tainted by Original Sin, but that at the close of her life in this world she ascended directly to the glory of heaven. This brings us to Prato, about eight miles north-west of Florence in Tuscany, which is the most famous of all European cities claiming to possess the girdle that, in apocryphal tradition, the Virgin Mary threw down to St Thomas at the Assumption. Even though the girdle has not left the city since it arrived from the East in the late eleventh century, its history has been eventful and strangely touched by sorrow and violence. In 1312 a thief who tried to steal it was put to a cruel death (he was burnt alive), and as late as 1767 a supposed threat to the relic led to rioting.[1]

The fundamental text for the cult at Prato is the account of the Assumption ascribed to Joseph of Arimathaea. This text was described by M. R. James as of Italian origin and no earlier than the thirteenth century. Although it exists in a late Welsh translation, it is predated by references in Welsh poetry, so that scholars now consider the girdle was already well known in Welsh oral tradition.[2] How well known it was is the subject of this chapter.

The reference by Iolo Goch (*c*.1320–1398) is the earlier of the two in Welsh poetry, neither of which mentions Prato.

> Degfed Tomas, hoywras hir,
> A'r India yw ei randir;
> Pan aeth Mair, fuddair addef,
> Gyda nifer Nêr i nef,
> O'i lleng hi a ollyngawdd
> O nef i Domas ei nawdd,
> Ei gwregys hi, wiw riain,
> Orau modd o aur a main;
> Hwnnw yw, iawnrhyw anrheg,
> Eu warant ef, wiw rent teg.[3]

Thomas is the tenth, his favour excellent and far-reaching, and his portion is India; when Mary (a blessed word to profess!) went with the Lord's host to heaven, from her host she let down to Thomas from heaven her protection, her girdle made most excellently of gold and jewels, the fair maiden. That is his security, a true gift, a fine proper repayment.

The second instance, quite secular in context, occurs in a love poem by Lewys Môn (*fl.* 1480–1527). He tells the girl:

> Os af yn dy ras hefyd,
> Ni wn baham yn y byd.
> Mair i Domas y cleiriach
> A roes ben ei gwregys bach:
> Mae'n dy fryd ymado fry,
> Moes em o'th wregys ymy.[4]

If too I progress in your favour, I do not know in the world why. Mary gave the tip of her little girdle to Thomas, a feeble

old man. You want to rise up and go; give me a jewel from
your girdle.

The tradition which the two bards used for their different purposes had been familiar since early times in the
Eastern Empire, particularly at Homs in Syria. But it seems
to have been unknown in the West much before the
twelfth century, like so many other Eastern influences.
After that we find associations of particular relics with
donors like Charlemagne or Edward the Confessor, at
places including Aachen, Maastricht, Wettingen (near
Baden in Switzerland), and Westminster. So it is in the late
twelfth century that evidence for the girdle in narrative
and art begins to multiply.[5]

The oldest surviving example of the theme in Western art
seems to be a thirteenth-century tympanum at Cabestany,
on the edge of the marshes between Perpignan and the
Mediterranean in south-west France. In discussing this,
Émile Mâle also mentioned an allegedly thirteenth-century
Italian miniature, but the authenticity of the latter has been
disputed. What seems to be the earliest Italian representation still extant is a painting of the late thirteenth century
(not the twelfth) at Spoleto, some twenty miles south of
Assisi. In it St Thomas runs to grasp with both hands a dark
cord held by the Virgin, who stands stiffly in a mandorla or
vesica piscis.* Her face has been destroyed.[6]

Other evidence is provided by a relief of the Virgin
giving the girdle to St Thomas, formerly on the south
portal of Strasbourg Cathedral. The relief, dated c.1230,
was destroyed in the French Revolution, but a drawing
survives. There is another thirteenth-century representation in the cathedral at Suzdal, about a hundred miles east-
north-east of Moscow, in the form of a drawing on copper
plate, serving as a reminder of the Eastern and Byzantine
origins of this devotion. So there is no shortage of material
for the the girdle in art, quite apart from that of Prato
itself, Florence, and Siena; instances from the fourteenth

---

* A pointed aureole in medieval sculpture and painting.

century include a fresco of 1313 at Snietogorsk, near Pskov on Russia's Estonian frontier, and a mural of 1317 at Staro Nagoricane, twenty-five miles north-east of Skopje in Macedonia.[7]

From the rich collection of later medieval art showing St Thomas receiving the girdle at the Assumption, associated (in varying degrees) with such names of Daddi, Orcagna, Agnolo Gaddi, Giotto (the Arena capel at Padua), Maso di Banco, Donatello, Filippo Lippi, Ghirlandaio, Sodoma, and Raphael, two examples may perhaps be picked out as of special significance. The first is a Tuscan fresco dated to between 1475 and 1489 in which a heavy-lidded Madonna sits, in a gown of pale pink, before a Thomas dressed in green and red. Besides her is a recumbent doe, and behind the recognizable form of Monte Morello, deep in shadow, a river and village before it. The serenity of this can be contrasted with one of the most festive of all pictures of the Assumption, an altarpiece by Matteo di Giovanni in the National Gallery. The Virgin ascends surrounded by tiers of gaily-dressed child angels, in pink, blue, or gold, all of them playing musical instruments (viol, psaltery, portative organ, a pair of kettledrums), or singing, while her pink girdle wriggles down to an astonished and unshaven St Thomas who, mouth open, is springing forward to catch it.[8]

The theme is familiar in Continental literary sources. The play of the Assumption in the York cycle can on this hence be referred to the fundamental instance in *Legenda Aurea* (iv. 241) of about 1250, and a fifteenth-century French play of the Assumption based upon it, but also to Italian narratives based on the pseudo-Joseph text mentioned above, examples in medieval Spanish and Italian drama, and a passage in the Middle High German poem *Assumptio Mariae*, written by Conrad of Heimesfurt in the early thirteenth century.[9]

Turning to the British Isles, we may first note that Westminster Abbey claimed to possess the girdle of the Virgin Mary in, according to an inventory of 1520, a 'long Coffre of Crystall'. This underwent something of a medieval odyssey in the track of various pregnant queens of England, as it was used to invoke the Virgin's protection when the dangerous moment of childbirth came. So in 1242 monks were sent off to Gascony with the girdle for the confinement of Queen Eleanor, again in 1338 to Antwerp for Queen Philippa, and once again for Philippa in 1355 to Woodstock. The Westminster monks remained at Antwerp for nearly six months, running up bills of which we still have a record. Although it was believed by the fifteenth century that the girdle had been given to the abbey by Edward the Confessor, its early history is obscure. Given the general history of the devotion, the influence of Osbert of Clare, who had a turbulent career as (for a time) prior of Westminster before he died in about 1160, may be significant here. Osbert was as zealous an advocate for the Immaculate Conception of the Blessed Virgin as he was for the canonization of the Confessor, writing tracts upon the first and going to Rome to advance the cause of the second. It would be as natural for such a relic to be acquired under his aegis as for it to be associated with the royal saint by the time John Flete (*fl.* 1421–65) wrote his history of the abbey.[10]

Carolyn Wall and Noel Ryan have also collected references to the girdle in Middle English literature. It seems the earliest that now survives is in a poem written in the south of England before 1250, although the oldest manuscript unfortunately does not contain the lines on the Assumption.

> A-bowte hure myddle a seynt [girdle] sche sought,
> That sche hure self hadde wrought,
> Off silk and gold wounden in pal [silk];
> Doun to thomas sche let it fal.
> He tok ther the gurdel in his honde,
> And thanked hure of hure sonde [gift].[11]

Warmer and more homely in its detail is a fourteenth-century variant version of the poem in the Auchinleck Manuscript.

Oure leuedi — blessed mote she be!
Of Thomas hadde gret pite,
In kare that was ibounde;
The gerdel of hire middel smal,
Nowt a gobet [part] therof, but al,
She let falle to grounde.[12]

Of the English mystery plays, only the York cycle still contains the play of the Blessed Virgin's Assumption (performed by the Weavers), the Chester play of the Assumption and Coronation having been lost. In the York play the Virgin declares to Thomas,

I schall the schewe
A token trewe,
Full fresshe of hewe,
My girdill, loo, take thame this tokyn.[13]

The play contains parts for twelve singing angels, whose music still exists. If the weavers were on their mettle in providing costumes for them and for the Virgin, York would have seen something of the splendour visible in Matteo di Giovanni's masterpiece in the National Gallery.

In the versions mentioned so far the girdle has usually been given to Thomas as a special grace because, being in India, he could not be present at the Assumption. In John Mirk's *Festial*, written at Lilleshall in east Shropshire before 1415, a different tradition appears, in which the girdle is given to overcome Thomas's otherwise invincible scepticism. Mirk imagines the Virgin rebuking the apostle in familiar terms: 'By that sonde of my gurdyll that I sende the, leue well that I am yn Heuen wyth my sonne, in body and in soule, as he ys.'[14] The episode of the girdle also figures in the English translation of *Legenda Aurea* published by Caxton in or after 1483.

Finally, the theme also occurs in medieval stained glass, embroidery, manuscript illumination, and sculpture, of which there is an important discussion in the *Corpus Vitrearum Medii Aevi* volume for Oxfordshire. The fact that so many of its comparative examples come from the

Oxford area suggests that others await discovery or rediscovery from the rest of Britain. The stained glass discussed is the fine example, dated to between about 1325 and 1350, from the church of the Assumption at Beckley, five miles north-east of Oxford. In it the Virgin appears as a pale, flaxen-haired maiden leaning from what looks like a great blanket held aloft by four angels. She hands down to Thomas a looped and braided girdle, of dark green, with a gold buckle at the end.

Other fourteenth-century examples of the theme occur in *opus Anglicanum* (the Syon cope in the Victoria and Albert Museum, and Pienza cope in Italy); manuscript illumination (New York, Pierpont Morgan Library, MS G.50, the 'De Lisle Hours'); wall-painting (at Broughton and Chalgrove, in north and south Oxfordshire respectively, and at Croughton in the southern tip of Northamptonshire); and stained glass (in the Stapleton chantry of North Moreton church, near Didcot, Oxfordshire). Of these examples the Chalgrove paintings are of special interest, showing Thomas not only receiving the girdle by the Virgin's tomb, but showing it later on at table to the other apostles.[15]

Besides these examples may be mentioned the striking roof boss (of the late fourteenth century) from the west porch of Peterborough Cathedral. Here the Virgin is a robed and bare-headed lady with long, loose-hanging hair who holds the girdle in her hand, with four crowned angels on surrounding bosses carrying respectively a shield, a palm, a psaltery, and a harp. The girdle, complete with buckle and clasp, is a stout strap as long as the Virgin is tall.[16]

It has been claimed that the theme of the girdle is common in English art only between 1290 and 1340 and in the later fifteenth century. Of the seventy or so English alabasters depicting the Assumption referred to in a standard study, alabasters found (thanks to medieval English exporters) from southern Spain to the Balkans, almost all belong to the later period. It is not clear how many include the detail of St Thomas and the girdle, though that at

Seville clearly does. St Thomas is generally shown as kneeling below the ascending Virgin, and holding the girdle over his arm or in his hand.[17]

At least one of these alabasters, apparently made at Burton-on-Trent, occurs in Wales, at Abergavenny. On the tomb of Richard Herbert (d. 1510), son of the Earl of Pembroke executed after the battle of Banbury in 1469, and father of the first Herbert Earl of Pembroke of the second creation, Richard is shown kneeling in plate armour, opposite his wife, below a representation of the Assumption. Behind Richard can be made out the figure of St Thomas, holding the girdle. Richard's elegy was written by Iorwerth Fynglwyd, so that he belongs to Celtic tradition in a way unusual for a grandee in late medieval England.[18]

In short, the theme shows the curious beliefs that can attach to Christian orthodoxy, whether one interprets that orthodoxy, like the characters of the novelist Pierre Morin in one of Graham Greene's short stories, as meaning 'at some point in history, somewhere in the latter years of the first century AD, the body of the Virgin had floated skywards, leaving an empty tomb', or that the holy body had rotted in the grave like other bodies.

After the Assumption, the Last Judgement, and the theme of the Virgin's rosary and St Michael's scales. The presence in Wales of this strange belief was noted long ago. 'In that Last Judgement when Michael weighed men's souls in the balance, it was given to Mary, men believed, to be at Christ's side, interceding for souls, weighing down the scales with her prayers against all the wiles of the evil one.'[19]

Few metaphors for human salvation and its opposite have been more insistent than that of the weighing of souls.[20] Although familiar from early Egyptian religion, it also appears in the ancient world from Greece to India; while the later association of the scales of judgement with St Michael, prince of heaven and captain of the angelic host, brought the archangel a cult that was famous and popular even by the standards of the Middle Ages, when one might think the cult of the saints reached its high water mark. Nevertheless, the present motif, of how the Virgin laid her rosary on the scales of St Michael, derives not from Coptic Egypt or Continental Europe (where it is unknown), but from medieval England, where it was common in painting and sculpture, contrasting with iconography elsewhere, in which the Virgin places on the balance her hand, a roll of *aves*, a candle, and so on.[21] As the evidence for it seems never to have been set out in detail, what appears below may interest iconographers as well as Celticists. The first may find it curious that, while the theme is apparently unknown in medieval English literature, it is common in Welsh. The second may wish to note how the bardic use of a theme (which must have been familiar throughout medieval Britain) gains perspective by comparison with the visual arts.

In Welsh there are at least eight examples of the theme, all dating from about 1450 onwards.

Pwyssaw n drwm ir kwm i kaid
   yn y dafl a wna dieflaid
Kael i minnau klaim uniawn
   baderau Mair lu drwm iawn
A phwys i wneuthur i hin
   oi llafur ai llaw Iessin.[22]

Devils in the scales press down heavily into the pit … but Mary's beads, a weighty company and load acting because of her labour and her fair hand, win me a just claim.

Although attributed to Iolo Goch, these lines come from verses by Hywel ap Dafydd ab Ieuan ap Rhys (active 1450–80) of Raglan.

Os roi esgus ry ysgon
Bid rol o baderau honn
Mawr yw bys Mair i bwyso
Nessa i Vair Annes a fo.[23]

If too slight an excuse be given, then may there be this rosary, because Mary's finger is strong to weigh down, and may the nearest to Mary be Anne.

Ieuan Deulwyn (active about 1460) of Kidwelly is here
trying to reconcile Rhys of Mabudrud (north of
Carmarthen) by reminding him of Judgement. 'Anne' may
be Rhys's wife, rather than St Anne, mother of the Virgin.

> Y phaderau am y pwysau a impysyd
> Ysgawnhae baich o'i llaw a'u braich
>   Nid llai i bryd [24]

The rosary was fixed about the scales, and her intent was not
less than to lighten the load from the scale beam with her
hand.

Gwilym Tew (active 1460–80) of Llangynwyd addresses
the Virgin of Penrhys, by the Rhondda Valley.

> Llun Mihangel a welwn
> A baiys a bwys hwnn
> Y gwr du yn hagr a dynn
> A llaw winau y llinyn
> A gafael yn i gyfair
> Drom iawn gan baderau mair
> Ar enaid yn farw yna
> Athro tost am weithred da
> El at Fair yfudd eirian
> Yntau ai wyr yn y tan
> At Fihangel pan elwyf
> Tynny berr Sattan i bwyf
> Ar f'enaid minau erfynwn
> Yn y pwys anap i hwnn
> Yn erbyn rhag ofn oerbair
> A wnel Mihangel a Mair.[25]

I saw the image of Michael and the sinner he weighs, and the
black Ugly One, tugging at the thread with his swarthy hand,
and the gripping on the other side, loaded down with Mary's
rosary; and the soul there, dying, teaching a sharp lesson
about good works. May Mary the meek and fair receive him;
in the fire, she knows. When I go to Michael, I shall tug
Satan's fork, and by my soul I shall wish ill luck in the scales!
May Michael and Mary, for fear of the icy cauldron, be
successful against him.

This comes from an unpublished poem by Llywelyn ap Hywel ab Ieuan ap Gronwy (active about 1480) of Llantrisant, Glamorgan.

> Mihangel, pan êl i'w naid
> Bes rhoen i bwyso'r enaid,
> Ni allo dim, o'r naill du,
> Dal pwys pwys, gyda help Iesu;
> Mae ar bwys Mair, a'i basiwn,
> Maddeu holl gamweddau hwn;
> Mam i thad, mamaeth ydych,
> Mair, saf gyda Morys wych,
> Par â bys pur i bwyso,
> Poed, ar bwys paderau, y bo![26]

When he comes to his judgement, O Michael, let them give it to weigh the soul! May nothing stop the weights on one side, with Jesu's help, because his passion and Mary's rosary can forgive all his sins. Mother of her father, you are a nurse, Mary; stand by fair Morys, have him weighed with a faithful finger, and be it, on a rosary's weight, as it may be!

Tudur's poem is an elegy for Morys ab Ieuan of Llangedwyn, in the Tanat valley west of Oswestry.

> Achos pan ddel yr enaid,
>   ar kythraulaid ar pwyse
> Maen bryderys ony chair,
>   gan vair ddodi phadere
> I gydbwyso an gelyn,
>   yn erbyn yn pechode.[27]

For when the soul comes, with the devils and the weights, it will be perilous unless Mary happen to place her rosary there, to outweigh our foe against our sins.

The lines are by Tomas ab Ieuan ap Rhys (*c*.1510–*c*.1560) of Tythegston, near Porthcawl.

An anonymous poem (presumbly of the fifteenth century) to the Virgin at Llanystumdwy, near Cricieth in north-west Wales, also mentions the tradition.

Pa son yn pwyso enaid
Oni cheir hon yn eich rhaid?
Pan weler ei phaderau
Yn troi am hyn yn trymhau,
Hwpo enaid heb poeni
I nef hwn a fynno hi ... [28]

Why mention the weighing of a soul, if you lack her in your need? When her rosary is seen turning about the tipping balance, may she desire this: to thrust soul painlessly into heaven.

Finally, the Virgin intercedes for the soul of a sinner in the play *Yr Elaid a'r Corff*, of the early sixteenth century, which was written for performance somewhere in Powys or north-east Wales.

Yrofyn yr wy gyda[g] e
I gael dodi fy mhadere.[29]

I ask that with him I may place my Pater Nosters.

That the theme was in no way restricted to Wales can be proved by a county list of examples (no doubt a small fraction of what once existed) of medieval English painting and sculpture. The writer was here helped by John Edwards (1913–98) of Oxford, who answered questions about the paintings listed below and provided information to exclude others. For more information, researchers should turn to Edwards's large collection of photographs, slides, books, and papers on medieval English wall-paintings, now deposited at the Courtauld Institute, London.

Buckinghamshire

St Lawrence, Broughton, a village now swallowed up by Milton Keynes. The *Victoria County History* describes the Virgin in the fifteenth-century wall-painting as 'extending her robe to shelter the saved, while with her left hand she gives a favouring touch to the beam of the balance in which a soul is being weighed. Round the beam is entwined a string of beads'.[30]

Cheshire

The Cathedral, Chester. A fragment of fifteenth-century stained glass, described as perhaps from a Last Judgement in the cathedral, and formerly belonging to the iconographer Philip Nelson, shows a rosary looped on part of a balance-beam above a soul in a scale-pan.[31]

Devon

St Peter, St Paul, and St Thomas of Canterbury, Bovey Tracey. A fifteenth-century wall-painting, now faded away, but known from a nineteenth-century copy, showed St Michael holding the scales while balancing on a vespertilian dragon with seven heads. Nearby, the Virgin sheltered souls under her cloak. A rosary substantially longer than she was tall led from her hands into the pan containing the saved soul.[32]

Hampshire

All Saints, Catherington. The church, in the South Downs a few miles north of Portsmouth, contains a wall-painting of about 1350, in which the Virgin holds the beam of St Michael's scale with her right hand. It is possible that she could formerly be seen placing a rosary on it with her left. What appears to be a rosary can be made out in the sketch published in one authority. However, other sources mention no rosary, the earliest of them merely descrbing the Virgin as having 'unhooked the scale containing the soul'.[33]

Kent

St Mary, Lenham, between Maidstone and Ashford. The church contains a wall-painting of about 1350 in which the

Virgin 'throws a rosary upon the balance beam' (Tristram). The other end of the beam has been seized by devils.[34] John Edwards informed the writer that the rosary was now not easy to see.

Lincolnshire

St John the Evangelist, Corby, a few miles north-east of Grantham. A wall-painting of the early fifteenth century, discovered in 1939, in which the Virgin is shown sheltering souls under her cloak between St Michael and the balance, 'placing the beads of her rosary on the right-hand end of the beam'. The protagonists are shown in clothes of reddish-brown, also the colour of the pattern stencilled in behind them.[35]

Norfolk

St Andrew, Wellingham. The village is some fifteen miles east of King's Lynn. In the painting of the weighing of souls on the rood screen the Virgin is shown 'adding her rosary to tip the balance'. The painting may be of the same date as another on the screen, of St George on horseback, dated 1532.[36]

Northamptonshire

All Saints, Croughton, in the southern tip of the county. The sole evidence for the Virgin's rosary in a fifteenth-century wall-painting of the Last Judgement is now a 'blank rosary-like shape on the downward balance-pan of the scales'.[37] But John Edwards, whose description is followed here, thought such a detail could well have been applied *in secco* once the rest of the painting had been finished, so that it would be the first part liable to disintegrate, especially after the removal of post-Reformation whitewash. He pointed out that this ghost rosary at Croughton would have parallels in Italian art.

All Saints, Nassington, near Oundle in the north-west of the county. A wall-painting of about 1400 which shows St Michael weighing souls with the 'balance beam weighed down by the rosary of the Virgin', which is looped over it.[38]

St Botolph, Slapton, three miles west of Towcester in the south of the county, contains a wall-painting of about 1350, in which the Virgin is described as resting her rosary 'on the right-hand pan of the scales', though the most recent commentator speaks rather of 'our Blessed Lady in red mantle and blue tunic, holding in her left hand a little box, and in her right a rosary which she is laying upon one end of the beam.'[39]

Oxfordshire

The Assumption of St Mary the Virgin, Beckley, on a hilltop five miles north-east of Oxford. The large and splendid wall-painting of the weighing of souls was largely destroyed in 1845. The drawing in the earliest account, based on the painting here and on that formerly at Islip, a few miles north, shows the Virgin casting her rosary onto the balance beam held by St Michael. Nothing now remains of the weighing of souls except one pan and part of a tapestry background.[40]

St Nicholas, Islip. A drawing of the destroyed wall-painting here, which seems to have resembled that at Beckley nearby, appeared in *The Gentleman's Magazine* in 1861, where the transcriber apparently did not recognize the rosary in the Virgin's right hand for what it was.[41]

St James, South Leigh, near Witney in west Oxfordshire, the scene of a Victorian art crime. The impressive and lively weighing of souls, in which the Virgin places her rosary on the beam of judgement, was shown by John Edwards to be entirely of 1872, and thus no sure guide to the original and much smaller weighing of souls now somewhere underneath it. But letters written at the time of the 'restoration' do establish that a rosary appeared in the original painting.[42]

St Peter and St Paul, Swalcliffe, five miles south-west of Banbury, has an elegant wall-painting of about 1400. The Virgin 'places her rosary in the scales' in it according to Caiger-Smith, though John Edwards informed the writer that this detail can no longer be seen.[43]

Somerset

St Michael, Minehead. A hillside church, one of the Michael churches of Ireland and west Britain. The weighing of souls appears in a freestone carving of the late fifteenth century on the outside of the tower, which the Virgin is represented as a *Schutzmadonna*, sheltering souls under her cloak, and 'laying her rosary on the beam' of the balance held by St Michael. The sculpture shows the influence of English alabasters on other media.[44]

Worcestershire

The Commandery or Hospital of St Wulstan, Worcester. The Virgin appears at the weighing of souls in one of a series of unusual paintings of the early sixteenth century, 'assisting with her rosary to balance the scale in the soul's favour'.[45]

Yorkshire

All Saints, Harewood, ten miles north of Leeds. A Gothic Valhalla. Amongst the aristocratic tombs in this chapel is one formerly identified as that of Sir John Neville of Oversley and his wife, but now thought to be that of Sir William Gascoigne (d. 1487) of Gawthorpe and his wife Margaret Percy. St Michael as weigher of souls appears as an alabaster weeper on the side of the tomb chest. The Virgin does not appear, but the scale pan containing the saved soul is weighed down by a rosary which must be hers.[46]

Besides the works of art listed above, the motif of the Virgin's rosary at the weighing of souls can be found in movable items, most obviously in English alabasters of the fifteenth century. These generally follow the pattern described above. In the English alabaster at Sampedor in north-east Spain, however, the Virgin is absent, and only the tassel of her rosary can be seen, hanging from one of the scale pans, a sophisticated detail comparable with that of the Harewood sculptures above.[47]

An instance of the theme in manuscript illumination, in a York Book of Hours (now Boulogne, Bibliothèque municipale, MS 93) of about 1390, has been discussed by Nicholas Rogers. On f. 24 appears 'St Michael holding scales, which the BVM tips by including a rosary, although devils endeavour to pull down the other side' (the last a detail often found elsewhere).[48]

The above show the immense popularity of the theme in medieval Britain, at both an aristocratic and a fairly humble level. Yet it is curious that it seems unknown in English literature before the account of God's Judgement, headed 'Wrath to Come', in *The Image of Both Churches* by John Bale (1495–1563). Bale spoke for the reaction of Protestant reformers, men 'zealous to remove every carved or painted trace of Mary-worship', of which few could be more abhorrent to them than this. Hence almost all our surviving evidence comes from wall-paintings (more easily whitewashed over than destroyed) in remote country parishes, and poems in a language of little interest to authority. Other forms of evidence were smashed or burnt. Bale thus declared,

> Just is he in his promise, true in his sayings, glorious in his works, holy, terrible, and fearful in his judgements against the wicked. None shall be found able at that day to restrain the least part of his purposed vengeance, neither Mary throwing her beads into St Michael's balance ... [49]

But the tradition of the Virgin's rosary and the scales was likewise suspect ('both churches' or not) to Catholic authority. The Flemish scholar Johannes Molanus or Jan Vermeulen (1533–1585), most influential theoretician of Counter-Reformation iconography, criticized medieval representations of the Last Judgement in these words:

> The Blessed Virgin will not then kneel before the Judge showing her breasts to plead for sinners ... But both the Blessed Virgin and the Blessed John will then be seated beside the supreme Judge in order that they may judge the world as assessors. At that time there will be no further room for mercy, as there is now, but only for justice.[50]

Virgin, rosary, and Judgement were in fact becoming an aspect of medieval belief beyond the recall of any modern church; and on this the last word may, perhaps, be left to a French critic.

> Dans la conception toute psychologique du jugement particulier adoptée aujourd'hui par la théologie, il n'y a plus de place pour un rôle effectif des anges ou des démons. On peut donc croire que ce sont là de simples figures pour enfoncer plus sûrement dans nos imaginations la réalité du jugement.[51]

Notes

1. Réau, ii/2, pp. 618, 621; vi, pp. 1267, 1270; Origo, p. 60; Hirn, pp. 55, 300–1, 394; Kirschbaum ii, col. 281, viii, col. 473.
2. James, pp. 216–18; Glanmor Williams, p. 101; Johnston, *Gwaith Iolo Goch*, p. 333.
3. Johnston, *Gwaith Iolo Goch*, pp. 110–11.
4. Rowlands, *Gwaith Lewys Môn*, p. 344.
5. Bock, pp. 11–14; Rauschen, p. 63; Beissel, pp. 295, 301; Willard, pp. 15–16; Folz, 178–9; Tschochner, 54.
6. Mâle, p. 256; Weiss, 13; van Os, pp. 154–6; Kaftal, cols 1080–2.
7. Weiss, 12–18; Gębarowicz, pp. 109–16, 202–4.
8. Borsook, pp. 113–15.
9. Carolyn Wall, 172–92.

10. Flete, p. 70; Westlake, pp. 80, 290, 295, 461, 499.
11. Lumby and McKnight, p. 133.
12. Breeze, 'Girdle', 98.
13. Beadle, p. 396.
14. Erbe, p. 225.
15. Caiger-Smith, pp. 71, 162, 165; Newton, p. 30.
16. Cave, p. 205; Pevsner and Metcalf, p. 284.
17. Cheetham, pp. 199–207.
18. Nelson, 'Some Fifteenth-Century Alabaster Panels', 136; H. Ll. Jones and E. I. Rowlands, pp. 30–1.
19. Glanmor Williams, p. 483.
20. Brandon, *passim*.
21. Tubach, no. 4180.
22. Johnston, *Gweithiau Iolo Goch*, p. 515.
23. Ifor Williams, *Casgliad*, p. 87.
24. G. J. Williams, p. 41.
25. Breeze, 'Virgin's Rosary', 91–2.
26. T. Gwynn Jones, pp. 323–4
27. Hartwell Jones, p. 453.
28. Ibid., p. 338; cf. Glanmor Williams, p. 491.
29. Gwen Jones, p. 250; cf. D. Simon Evans, pp. 53–4.
30. Caiger-Smith, p. 63; Breeze, 'Virgin's Rosary', 93.
31. Nelson, 'Some Unusual English Alabaster Panels', 86.
32. Breeze, 'Virgin's Rosary', 93.
33. Borenius and Tristram, p. 38.
34. J. C. Wall, p. 191; Tristram, p. 191; Caiger-Smith, p. 152.
35. Caiger-Smith, pp. 29, 152.
36. Williamson, p. 343.
37. Caiger-Smith, p. 162.
38. Tristram, p. 225; Caiger-Smith, pp. 62, 163.
39. Tristram, p. 247; Caiger-Smith, p. 164; Chapman, p. 12.
40. Caiger-Smith, p. 164.
41. Breeze, 'Virgin's Rosary', 95.
42. Caiger-Smith, p. 168; Edwards, 'A "Fifteenth-Century" Wall-Painting', 131–42.
43. Caiger-Smith, p. 61.
44. Cheetham, p. 49.
45. Moore, pp. 282–3
46. Routh, pp. 56, 60; Routh and Knowles, pp. 34–5.
47. Hildburgh, pp. 129–31; Cheetham, pp. 49, 133–4.
48. Rogers, 38.
49. Christmas, p. 523.
50. Woolf, p. 124 n. 2
51. Quoted in Breeze, 'Virgin's Rosary', 97.

The Praise of the Virgin

In the first century AD, Mary's life on earth came to its close; at some date in the early second century there died the last person to have known her. But this was not, of course, the end. *Beatam me dicent omnes generationes*, 'all generations will call me blessed', so that she is now praised all over the world 'continually, without interruption'; and the Second Vatican Council, in its constitution *Lumen Gentium*, comments on how after the Council of Ephesus in 431 there was 'a remarkable growth in the cult of the people of God towards Mary, in veneration and love, in invocation and imitation, according to her own prophetic words: "all generations will call me blessed, for he who is mighty has done great things for me".'[1]

In this tide of praise Wales has its place. Some poets, using terms from ancient Roman poetry, call her a rose among thorns; others set out her joys and sorrows; others again sing of her wonders in phrases that find their analogies in Jewish or medieval Latin sources, or even nursery rhymes.

We begin with the theme of Mary, rose amongst thorns. In 1993 the writer argued that five early Welsh poems, including three in the thirteenth-century Black Book of Carmarthen, can be attributed to a Master John mentioned in eight St Davids documents, the early not before 1148, the latest not after 1176.[2] These poems hence offer precise information on Marian learning and devotion at St Davids in the later twelfth century.

One aspect of this is a passage on the rose amongst thorns in a didactic and celebratory poem beginning 'Goruchel Duw, golochir ym pobva', the so-called 'Difreg-wawd Taliesin'. Despite its title, it has nothing to do with the bard Taliesin (who predated Master John by nearly six centuries). This psalm of praise apparently shows Master John's knowledge of *Carmen Paschale* by the fifth-century poet Caelius Sedulius, and specifically of his imagery of roses.

Through medieval Europe the rose was a symbol of the Virgin. This has a scriptural origin in Song of Solomon 2:1–2 (Douay version), 'I am the flower of the field, and the lily of the valleys. As the lily among thorns, so is my love among the daughters.' The 'flower of the field' here was interpreted as the Virgin Mary from Fortunatianus of Aquileia (d. before 371) onwards. Identification of the Virgin as an actual rose came later, in part through Ecclesiasticus 24:18, 'I was exalted like a palm tree in Cades, and as a rose plant in Jericho.'[3] These biblical references, together with the influence of Christian Latin poets like Sedulius, enabled the Virgin Mary to acquire the name of the rose from about the year 400 onwards.

The Marian rose cult takes various forms. In English it appears in the fourteenth-century alliterative poem *Cleanness*, which at line 1079 declares how with the Nativity there was rose scent where rottenness had always been (*And ther watz rose reflayr where rote hatz ben euer*), and, at its simplest, in the opening lines of the fifteenth-century carol, 'Ther is no rose of swych vertu, / As is the rose that bar Jhesu.'[4] More complex treatment links the Marian rose with Isaiah 11:1, 'And there shall come forth a rod out of the root of Jesse: and a flower shall rise up out of his root', familiar from the German hymn, '*Es ist ein ros' entsprungen / Aus einer Wurzel zart*.'[5]

However, the aspect of the rose cult discussed below associates flower and thorns. Sometimes the Virgin is called *rosa sine spina*, as in the thirteenth-century carol 'Of on that is so fayr and bright'.[6] Elsewhere the Virgin is called *rosa inter spinas*, and this is itself developed in various ways. In the antiphon *Solem iustitiae, regem paritura supremum*, Fulbert of Chartres (*c*.975–1029) identified the thorns as the Jews: *Sicut spina genuit Iudaea Mariam*. The same idea occurs in the Christmas hymn, *Salve, festa dies, toto venerabilis aevo* by Hildebert of Lavardin (1056–1133).[7] The anti-Semitic use of the image was given an unexpected twist by the Spanish poet and rabbi, Sem Tob (?1290–1369), who said the rose was worth no less for being born on a thornbush, or good examples any less because a Jew gave them.[8]

In *Salve, mater salvatoris* by Adam of St Victor (*c*.1110–*c*.1180), the thorns are sin, from which the Virgin Mary is free: *Sed tu spinae nescia*.[9] But in a third variant of the *rosa inter spinas* motif the thorns stand for Eve. It is Master John's use of this in *Goruchel Duw, golochir ym pobva* that concerns us here. After beginning his poem with praise of God, Master John goes on to outline the nature of the universe, including the six ages of history. The last of these ages is that of Jesus, who came with his mother 'as there came from thorns the flowers of the rose'.

Cyntaf oes: oes Adaf ac oes Eua;
Eiloes: oes Noë, a nofyes yn y archa;
Tryded oes: oes Abraham, penn ffyd, pater patriarcha;
Pedwared oes: oes Moessen ym Mynyd Syna
Pan gauas degeir dedyf yn y dir westua;
Pymhet oes: oes detwyd Dauyd propheta;
Chwechet oes: oes Iessu, a hyt Vrawt y para,.
Ac yndi y prouet y prophessya:
Y doeth o epil ennwir Eua,
Mal y daw ar y drein, blodeu rosa.
Meir Wyry doeth o uru Anna,
A Iessu a dyuu o vru Maria.[10]

The first age, the age of Adam and age of Eve; the second age, the age of Noah, who floated in his Ark; the third age, the age of Abraham, lord of faith, father-patriarch; the fourth age, the age of Moses on Mount Sinai, when he received the ten commandments in his sure dwelling; the fifth age, the joyous age of David the prophet; the sixth age, the age of Jesus, and it will last until Doomsday. And in that age prophecy was fulfilled: he came from the sinful line of Eva as there come from thorns the flowers of the rose. The Virgin Mary came from the womb of Anna, and Jesus came from the womb of Mary.

The poem was widely read. Unfortunately, the texts vary greatly, with that in the Red Book of Hergest of *c*.1400 already showing corruption. The poem is almost invariably ascribed to Taliesin, where the spurious title *Difregwawd Taliesin*, his 'flawless song', suggests how the poem's learning led to this, the bard having gained a reputation in the Middle Ages as an omniscient necromancer, a Celtic equivalent to medieval Vergil.

Yet the reference to the Virgin as Eve's descendant thus has nothing to do with bardic magicians. It suggests Master John's source for the image of the rose was Sedulius's *Carmen Paschale* (*c*.430), where the simile's Marian context is clear.

> Et velut a spinis mollis rosa surgit acutis,
> Nil quod laedat habens matremque obscurat honore:
> Sic Evae de stirpe sacra veniente Maria,
> Virginis antiquae facinus nova virgo piaret.[11]

> And as the tender rose springs from sharp thorns, and has nothing that harms or conceals the honour of the stem, so likewise is Holy Mary coming from the line of Eve, that the new virgin might atone for the evil of the ancient one.

Sedulius based the lines on Vergil's *Eclogue* V, 38–9 (as its editor points out), though he borrows words rather than concepts. Vergil reverses the roles of soft and sharp; refers to violet, not rose; and speaks of land become wilderness, rather than thorn and rose in one plant: *Pro* molli *viola, pro purpureo narcisso, / Carduus et* spinis surgit paliurus acutis. The reshaping of Vergil's theme, and its brilliant application to the contrast of Eve and Mary (made as early as Justin Martyr and St Irenaeus of Lyon in the second century), may be due to Sedulius himself.

How does Master John's use of Sedulius fit into the Latin culture of early Britain? The first point to note here is that the knowledge of cosmology, geography, scripture, exegesis, grammar, Latin, Greek, and Hebrew shown in Master John's poems, together with his title of 'master', indicates that he was a product of the schools. If so, his familiarity with *Carmen Paschale* would be no surprise, as it was a stock text of medieval education. It was used in a Hiberno-Latin commentary on St Mark, attributed to Cummianus, perhaps Abbot of Clonfert (in modern County Galway), and author of a letter to Abbot Ségéne of Iona on the date of Easter.[12] It also influenced the Hiberno-Latin *Hisperica Famina* of about 650.[13] Aldhelm and Bede knew it thoroughly, and Bede actually comments on Aldhelm's verse and prose *De Virginitate* as 'a twofold work after the example of Sedulius', like Bede's own *Life of St Cuthbert*.[14] Sedulius is quoted in the poems of an otherwise unknown Æthilwald (pupil of Aldhelm) in Vienna, Österreichische Nationalbibliothek, MS 751 (Theol. 259).[15] Between 716 and 731, Bishop Cuthwine of *Domnoc* (Felixstowe in Suffolk, and *not* Dunwich farther north) owned an illuminated manuscript of *Carmen Paschale*, based on an Italian original; a ninth-century copy of Cuthwine's book from St Jacques, Liège, is now Antwerp, Museum Plantin-Moretus, MS 126.[16] An eighth-century English text of *Carmen Paschale*, with tenth-century Old English glosses, is bound up with the Parker Chronicle and Laws in Cambridge, Corpus Christi College, MS 173.[17] In a life of St Willibrord, Alcuin followed Sedulius, Aldhelm, and Bede in writing verse and prose versions of the same material. Alcuin also mentions Sedulius as an author in the York library, in its day the finest north of the Alps (and entirely destroyed by the Danish conquest in 866, except apparently for one Noah, a Cassiodorus now at Durham).[18] Asser quotes ten lines from *Carmen Paschale*, perhaps amongst his reading at St Davids, in his life of King Alfred.[19]

That Sedulius was read by ninth-century Bretons as well as by Welshmen is shown by nine Old Breton glosses in Orleans, Bibliothèque municipale, MS 302 (255).[20] In the later tenth century *Carmen Paschale* was copied, possibly at Worcester, in what is now Oxford, Bodleian Library, MS lat. theol. c.4. This, a fragment of four folios from 'a fine and large copy of Sedulius', was discovered in the fifteenth-century binding of a Reading manuscript. A Welsh link of the Bodleian fragment is implied by a gloss* hand in it which, according to Bishop, resembles one in Cambridge, University Library, Ff.4.42 (a manuscript of Juvencus in ninth-century Welsh minuscule). In Juvencus the hand (presumably Bradshaw's hand G, of the tenth or eleventh century) left 111 Welsh glosses and nine Irish ones. It seems the glossator** was a Welsh-speaking Irishman, one of three such who glossed the manuscript between the nine and eleventh centuries, possibly at St Davids, where Irish influence was long established. Perhaps about the year 1000 an Irish glossator, having studied Juvencus at St Davids, went to study Sedulius at Worcester. The hand in any case suggests the similarity of curriculum in English and Welsh monastic schools at that date, and the presence in an English school of a scribe trained in a Welsh scriptorium.[21]

The beginning of a hymn by Sedulius is quoted in the life of St Oswald of York by Bryhtferth, writing at Ramsey Abbey (near Peterborough) between 995 and 1005.[22] *Carmen Paschale* was amongst poetry bequeathed by Leofric to Exeter Cathedral, together with Persius, Statius, Prudentius, Arator, and the Exeter Book.[23] Another copy of it was written in about 1050, probably at St Augustine's Abbey, Canterbury, in what is now Cambridge, University Library, MS Gg.5.35, a classbook famous for its collection of Latin lyrics from the Rhineland, the 'Cambridge Songs'. The manuscript seems originally to have consisted of three classbooks with authors set out in order of difficulty. Juvencus as easiest comes first, Sedulius second, then

* Gloss: a note added to a text, usually to translate or explain a foreign or unusual word.
** Glossator: one who adds glosses to a text.

Arator, Tiro Prosper, Prudentius, Lactantius, Boethius, and so on.[24] Leland mentions a copy of Sedulius which he saw at Sherborne, Dorset.[25]

The importance of Sedulius as a school text is shown not only by glosses in English, Welsh, Irish, and Breton in various manuscripts, and by MS Gg.5.35, in which *Carmen Paschale* is presented as elementary study, but (somewhat unexpectedly) by letters of Herbert Losinga. A former Abbot of Ramsey, Herbert continued to teach even when Bishop of Norwich c.1095–1119, and while away from the cloister wrote to former pupils, providing glimpses of his schoolroom. Letters to William and Otto, boys to whom he had taught Donatus, show him vexed to hear they were reading Sedulius. He tells them Sedulius is a heavy diet suitable for more mature monks, comparing him with the Gospels (whose treatment of the same matter he preferred). Boys do better on the milk of much lighter literature (he recommends Ovid).[26]

In short, the evidence shows that Sedulius was not just a staple author of the medieval curriculum, like Arator, Juvencus, and Prudentius, but that he was 'easily the most popular' of them.[27] His high reputation in the Middle Ages contrasts with the modern view of him as all too like the 'inflated, vain, soulless, and unintelligent rhetors' Fulgentius and Enodius; a poet who could take the 'frippery of the pagan school rhetor', make it into Christian clothing, and 'strut about in it'.[28]

Evidence for the knowledge of Sedulius in early Britain is here set out to show him as a likely source for a St Davids scholar, and also to supplement an account of rose-imagery and the Blessed Virgin by Peter Dronke, who emphasizes the role in it of classical Greek lyric and a Carolingian Latin translation of *Hymnos Akathistos*, which 'helped to bring on the great stream of flower and rose imagery devoted to the Virgin in the West'.[29] *Pace* Dronke, Sedulius must, nevertheless, have also spread Marian rose-imagery in the West long before and after Charlemagne's time.

An apostrophe to the Virgin in an anonymous sermon

adds to evidence for the image of the rose amongst thorns in the fifth century: *O rosa inter spinas, lilium inter tribulos, apis inter volucres, gemma inter lapides!* This figures in a sermon (of the fifth or sixth century?) in Montpellier, Faculté de Médecine, MS 59, a homiliary of the late ninth or tenth century. The sentence, in an otherwise banal sermon, nonplussed its editor, who remained guarded on the question of its origin. While not discounting influence from the Eastern Empire, Barré considered inspiration for it more likely to be scriptural, though noting Sedulius's use of the image at about the same date.[30] The theme in this sermon may be compared with the influence of *Carmen Paschale* in the hymn *Ave, caeli ianua,* of the tenth century or later. This occurs in a tenth-century hymnal (now in the Vatican) traditionally linked with Moissac (near Toulouse), though in fact from the Abbey of Saint Martin de Montauriol. Later versions of the hymn occur in a Reims manuscript now at Bern, and a processional in the cathedral library at Lucca.[31]

What conclusions does this wealth of material on Sedulius and Master John point to? There are three. The theme of Mary as the rose was known in the West long before the Carolingian revival. We can be sure as well that Sedulius was read at St Davids in the twelfth century as Asser and the Juvencus glosses imply he was in the ninth and tenth. Finally, it provides a striking instance in the vernacular poetry of Britain before 1200 of a loan from Latin poetry in the classical tradition (which specifically echoes Vergil). With the other evidence for Master John's reading, it indicates a range of learning unusual for an Insular Latin poet at that date.

Here we turn from the old Roman poets and their inheritors to a theme which is characteristically medieval, that of the Blessed Virgin's Joys and Sorrows. In poetry of that date the subject is universal. The joys are perhaps most familiar to medievalists from lines 646–7 of *Sir Gawain and the Green Knight*: 'The fyue joyez / That the hende Heuen Quene had of hir Chylde'. But they were equally well known in the rest of Christendom. In Spain, for example, they appear in the thirteenth-century *Milagros de Nuestra Señora* of Gonzalo de Berceo, the fourteenth-century *Libro de Buen Amor* of Juan Ruiz, and the fifteenth-century poems of Íñigo López de Mendoza, marqués de Santillana.

So it is no surprise to find the Virgin's joys and sorrows in medieval Welsh and Irish poetry. In Welsh the five earthly joys are listed twice. The first instance occurs in a religious poem attributed in the Red Book of Hergest to Bleddyn Ddu (*c.*1200), but to Rhisierdyn (*fl.* before 1382) in Aberystwyth, National Library of Wales, MS Peniarth 118. The second is a poem on the Virgin by Dafydd ab Edmwnd (*fl.* 1450–90), which also lists the Virgin's five earthly sorrows and five heavenly joys. Other allusions to the Virgin's joys and sorrows occur in Welsh secular poetry.

These two Welsh poems on the Virgin can be matched by at least one other in Irish, a poem on her five sorrows attributed to Donnchadh Mór Ó Dálaigh, though it has so far been unclear whether this refers to the celebrated Donnchadh Mór (d. 1244) described by the Four Masters as 'a poet who never was and never will be surpassed', or a lesser Donnchadh Mór writing before 1400.

Certain features of these three lyrics in Irish and Welsh seem to be unique in any Insular vernacular. What appears here thus not only tries to place the origins and circulation of these Marian themes within an international context, but attempts to show how sources in other vernaculars and Latin can be used to date poetry in the Celtic languages.

In what follows, therefore, these three points are argued. First, comparison with material in English, Latin, and Anglo-Norman suggests the Red Book poem is hardly as old as 1200; it is hence most unlikely to be by Bleddyn Ddu; it is thus probably by the fourteenth-century Anglesey poet Rhisierdyn.

Second, Dafydd ab Edmwnd's poem is related to other medieval texts on the Virgin's joys and sorrows, including the Latin hymn *Gaude virgo laus cunctorum*. It is suggested that the last part of his poem is his translation of the Latin hymn, the work of the fourteenth-century Austrian Cistercian, Christan von Lilienfeld. If so, the poetry of late medieval Wales would contain unusual evidence for contacts between Welsh literary culture and the poetic and religious life of central Europe.

Third, other evidence for the sorrows is used to show that the Irish poem can hardly date from the thirteenth century. If the attribution can be trusted, it must be by a later Donnchadh Mór, a County Clare poet writing towards the end of fourteenth century.

When we turn to the Red Book poem, we find that the problem of its dating has to be set against the history of the devotion to the Virgin's five joys, for which the first evidence seems to be a Latin poem written at Canterbury about 1050. It is worth noting that much of the earlier material on the joys (that is, written before 1200) is English, though the devotion was also known in eleventh-century Italy. It seems that at some date in the (late?) twelfth century, in the hymn *Gaude virgo mater Christi*, the joys were first set out as the specific five of Annunciation, Nativity, Resurrection, Ascension, and Assumption.[32] In the thirteenth century these five first appear in the vernacular, in *Ancrene Wisse*, a rule for anchoresses perhaps written in north Herefordshire between 1215 and 1221, or possibly a little later.[33] The same joys also appear in three thirteenth-century English lyrics.[34] These English and Latin texts may be compared with the passage on the joys from the Red Book of Hergest poem.

Coeth Ueir uawrvreint	ar y chreivyeint,	wir y chreuyd,
Kauas o'e naf	bom llawenaf	bump llewenyd.
Kyntaf ry vu —	reit y'n kanvu,	rat a'n kenuyd,
Kennelw a'n gwnel —	kennat Abriel,	kanneit, wybryd.
Dawn arwyre	dywawt aue,	dauawt ufyd;
Didwyll wrthi	Duw y cheli	vu y chilyd.
Eil urdedic	duw nydolic,	ny didolyd,
Gan enryded	gein ediued,	geni Douyd.
Lleuuer kyfyawn,	llawn o'r tridawn,	llyna'r trydyd:
Lle yd anregwyt	Duw an proffwyt,	dewin prif ffyd.
Llewych uab Meir,	rat bit wireir	reit bedweryd.
Llyw Sudea	ac wyr Anna	o gerennyd,

Gwedy daruot	odeu hynot	y dihenyd,
Gwenergweith dymp	yr gras arwymp	ar groes irwyd —
O vrat Judas	byt alanas	bu dilonyd,
A brawt Bilat,	ynat afrat,	eneit efryd —
Cof gogonet	vn trwy dytwet,	an tri detwyd,
Kyuodi Naf	o'r lle issaf	yr lluossyd.
Pymhet diffael	kyfarchauael,	kyfeirch ufyd,
Pan ysgynnawd,	arawt atrawd,	eureit etryd.
Nerth a bara,	y sant wylua	a seint eluyd,
Ner brenhinawl,	Naf achedawl,	nef uchedyd.
O'r byt pan aeth	mawr dewinyaeth	Meir diwenyd
Doeth niuer kein	y gael arwein	y gelorwyd —
Duw a'e deulu	y gyfleu	yn gyfluyd
Corff bendigeit	a hy eneit	Meir huenyd;
Caryat gleindit	nef y gelwit	yn digelwyd.[35]

Pure Mary of great nobility for her forgiveness, true her faith, gained from her Lord — may we be most joyful — five joys. The first was — necessity found us, grace will find us, may it make us refuge — the message of Gabriel, radiant, cloudy. He with the gift of raising from the dead said 'Ave' with humble tongue; sincere towards her, the Lord her God was her companion.

A second time honoured, on Christmas Day the birth of the Lord with honour (handsome heir) does not set her apart.

Righteous light, full of the three gifts — that was the third — when there were bestowed gifts to God our prophet, seer of foremost faith.

Light, son of Mary, grace is the true word of the fourth need. The ruler of Judaea, and by kinship Anna's grandson, after his death occurred (strange purpose), on Friday's appointed time for fair grace on the life-giving Cross (from Judas's treason carnage to the world that was without easing, and the judgement of Pilate, evil judge, crippled soul) — memory of glory, One through the earth, our Three fortunate ones(?) — the resurrection of the Lord from the lowest place for the sake of the hosts.

A fifth unfailing, the Assumption, humble greetings, when she ascended, praise that is sung, to her glorious home, the host that endures, the holy feast day and the saints of the world — to the royal Lord and generous master, to the high one of heaven.

When blessed Mary went from the world, great the prophecy, a fair company came to bear away her bier; the blessed body and brave soul of radiant Mary, of pure love, were called to heaven by God and his host, truly to be placed amongst a multitude.

This Welsh passage, unlike the Latin and English texts cited above, includes the Epiphany as the third joy and leaves out the Ascension. Now, if the passage dated from about 1200, this would be remarkable, because no other example of the five joys which includes the Epiphany can be dated much before about 1275, and the really popular period for this devotion is the fourteenth century. Neither the Latin instances (in a copy of Gobi's *Scala Caeli* in Prague, University Library, MS XIII E 3 A, and a poem in London, British Library, MS Royal 7 A. vi, from Durham) nor those in English (in the Göttingen *Cursor Mundi* and the Harley Lyrics) occur in a manuscript pre-dating the fourteenth century, and even the earliest example, in an Anglo-Norman lyric, cannot be dated much earlier than the last quarter of the thirteenth.[36]

For this reason the ascription of the Red Book poem to Bleddyn Ddu, writing about 1200, should be rejected. If the poem really were as early as this, it would not only be the earliest vernacular text in Europe to enumerate the five joys, but would be almost as old as the earliest text listing the five joys, the hymn *Gaude Virgo Mater Christi* (which cannot be its source, as the two poems differ in the joys listed and the style in which they are described). Further, the Welsh poem would predate by the best part of a century any other text mentioning the Epiphany amongst the five joys. But if we attribute the verses to the Gwynedd bard Rhisierdyn, these difficulties disappear, and the passage falls into place with all others in lyrics celebrating the Epiphany amongst the joys.

No other reference in Welsh to the five joys redates the

fifteenth century. But after 1450 the evidence is for a devotion only too familiar. So much we learn from an erotic
poème noir, attributed to Robin Ddu (active about 1450) of
Anglesey, which mocks the Virgin Mary, the Virgin's
mother St Anne, the Old Testament, and the Mass. The
bard says of the girl that her eyes are like bright brooches,
her skin is as white as that of 'St Anne's niece', her handsome body makes him lapse from his faith, and her smile
is the five joys:

Dy wên yw'r pum llawenydd.[37]

More conventional is a praise-poem to Siôn Hafard of
Pontwilym, near Brecon, where Lewys Glyn Cothi (active
1447–86) declares of this obscure young man that his
poetic gift contains the five books of Moses, and that one
of his words is worth the five joys of Mary:

Pum llawenydd Mari dros ungair Siôn.[38]

Elsewhere Lewys describes the patron Gruffydd Derwas,
of the great house of Nannau above the Mawddach
estuary in mid-Wales, as his 'five joys':

Llyna i'm bump llawenydd.[39]

A fourth poem, a catalogue of fives in an elegy by Gwilym
ab Ieuan Hen (active 1440–80), praises the five sons of
Dafydd ap Tomas of Llandyfrïog, near Newcastle Emlyn
in Dyfed, by ransacking the universe for fives (he
compares these young men to them).[40]

Another poem, by Gutun Owain (active 1460–98) of
Dudleston, near Oswestry in Shropshire, is of special
interest for the poem by Dafydd ab Edmwnd quoted
below, because it mentions the Virgin's sorrows as well as
her joys. In this poem, an elegy for Abbot Siôn ap Rhisiart
of Valle Crucis (near Llangollen in the Dee Valley), Gutun
says of the dead abbot (modifying Robin Ddu's phrase?):

I wên 'vv'r pvm llywennydd
Ar veirdd, a'r pvm pryder 'vydd.[41]

His smile was the five joys for poets, and it will be the five
sorrows.

But by far the most interesting examples of the themes
occur in a poem on the Four Daughters of God and the
Virgin's Five Joys, Five Sorrows, and Five Triumphs by
the poetry and gentleman Dafydd ab Edmwnd (active
1450–90). This great master of the Welsh language was
born and is buried at Hanmer, Flintshire. His poem must
have been popular, since it survives in more manuscripts
than anything else he wrote. According to the Elizabethan
parson David Johns of Llanfair Dyffryn Clwyd, Dafydd
wrote the poem overnight on a test subject set by the
magnate Gruffudd ap Nicolas at the Carmarthen
eisteddfod of 1453: 'pan erchis Gruffyth ap Nicolas ir
prudyddion wneythur un bob un erbyn tranoeth pan fu r
eisteddfod ynghaer fyrddin'.[42] It won Dafydd first prize (a
badge with the device of a silver chair on it). Dafydd's
poem deserves its popularity and its chair for the skill,
directness, and honesty of its expression. But it possesses
other features which heighten its interest and make it in
some ways unique.

After beginning his poem with the praise of the Four
Daughters of God, Dafydd turns to the Blessed Virgin's
five earthly joys:

Un fu gael o Nef Geli
Y sôn a'i beichioges hi.
A'r ail nwyf o'r lan ofeg
Oedd eni Duw i'r ddyn teg.
Da oedd i'w fam, trydydd fu
Duw Sul gyfodi Iesu.
Pedwerydd o'i ddydd oddef
Pan aeth y mab byw i nef.
A'r pumed fu'r mynediad
Am ei dwyn lle mae ei Dad.[43]

One was gaining from God's heaven the word by which she conceived, and the second joy from pure intent was the birth of God to the fair one. The third — good was it for his mother — was Jesus's resurrection on Sunday. The fourth because of her son's day of favour, when he ascended alive to heaven; and the fifth was the journey, her being brought to the place where his Father is.

Dafydd's account of the joys is so straightforward that one cannot name a source for it, and no doubt he needed none. He uses the same sequence for the five joys as his many English comtemporaries, though he excels them in the distinction and clarity of his language.

Dafydd goes on to list the Virgin's five sorrows:

pryder mair prydir yw modd
pryd arall i pryderodd
vn braw aeth yni bron
o rysymol air simon
a ffan golles yr jessu
alaeth yw vam eilwaith vv
duw a welai mewn dolur
drwy i chwsc weldyna dri chur
pedwar galar am geli
pann vv ar groes peonvawr gri
pymed oedd weled i ddwyn
mor varw ar vraich mair vorwyn[44]

At another time Mary felt grief, a sorrow to her countenance. One fear entered her breast from Simeon's wise word; and when she lost Jesus, his mother felt grief a second time. In her sleep she saw God in anguish, and that is three sorrows. The fourth grief concerning God was the cry of agony when he was on the Cross; the fifth, to see him carried stark dead on the Virgin Mary's arm.

It is remarkable that the passage above seem to be the only one on the Virgin's sorrows in the vernacular poetry of medieval Britain. There is certainly nothing else on the subject amongst our approximately 5900 surviving lyrics in Middle English. All we have in English are instances in prose and the evidence for a lost poem (noted below) on this theme. It is a comment on the gaps in our knowledge of literature in Britain and Ireland that proof for the five sorrows in poetry should survive in Welsh and Irish, but not in the majority language, English.

The history of this devotion was set out by Dom André Wilmart, who considered five was probably the original number of sorrows, even though in Europe as a whole five is less common than seven or fifteen. Wilmart defined what he called the *série commune* of five sorrows (Simeon's prophecy, the loss of the boy Jesus, Christ's arrest, crucifixion, and deposition), of which only traces survive. He referred to instances of it in the Grandes Heures de Rohan (Paris, Bibliothèque nationale, MS lat. 9471), produced at Paris, and *Analecta Hymnica*. All these instances date from the fifteenth century.[45]

However, the same five sorrows can be found slightly earlier, in a legend of the Christ and the Virgin which had international currency in the Middle Ages, but later fell foul of the Inquisition. The legend describes the promises Christ made to the Virgin for anyone who honours her five sorrows. Wilmart cited a version of the legend in English from London, British Library, MS Add. 37787, a miscellany (containing many English lyrics) which in 1386 belonged to a novice of Bordesley Abbey, in north-east Worcestershire. Wilmart also mentioned a version of the legend in British Library, MS Add. 19909. The story achieved wider circulation when John Herolt (d. 1468), a Nuremberg Dominican, incorporated it as miracle twelve in his *Promptuarium de Miraculis Beatae Mariae Virginis*, especially after the advent of printing, when Herolt's works were often republished well into the sixteenth century. But with the coming of the Counter-Reformation there was a reaction, attested by early copies of *Promptuarium* in Pamplona libraries, where this passage, *expurgado conforme a los expurgaciones de los años 1640 y 1707*, is inked out.

Although the theme does not now survive in Middle English poetry, there is some evidence that it was known there, as Rosemary Woolf argued on the basis of the Bordesley manuscript, where the legend was clearly related to a *Planctus Mariae* (now almost entirely lost) preceding it. However, a prose example of the devotion without the legend does occur in Lincoln, Cathedral Library, MS 91, the so-called 'Thornton Manuscript' compiled about 1440 for Robert Thornton of East Newton, near Helmsley, some twenty-two miles north of York:

> Now dere lady, for the perturbance thou thou hade whene Symeone sayde to the, 'The swerde of sorowe', he said, 'sall passe thorowte thyne awnne saule': preye thy dere sone to helpe me ... for the sorowe thou hade when thi sone was loste fra the thre dayes & thou soughte hym with gretande hert: preye thy sone to gyffe me contrycioune ... for the sorowe thou thou hade whene that thou wiste in spyryte that thi sone was tane & solde thole the dede: pray thi sonne to delyuer me ... for the sorowe that thou hade whene that thou saughe thy dere sone hynge one the Crosse with freche wondys newe-made, rede with his awnne blode: preye thy blyssede sone to make me birnande in his luffe ... for the sorowe that thou hade whene that thi dere sone laye dede in thyne armes: preye thi sone to saffe me fra dampnacyoune ... [46]

The above material, together with Donnchadh Mór's poem below, proves that Dafydd ab Edmwnd's listing of the Virgin's sorrows was part of a devotion familiar in England, Ireland, and the rest of Europe. One other feature of the passage in Dafydd's poem calls for comment; the legend of the Virgin's dream, in which she saw the arrest at Gethsemane. This can be compared with the Thornton text, which speaks of the Virgin's knowing of the arrest *in spyryte*, and the Irish and Latin material discussed below. The tradition also figured in medieval Welsh drama, and survived in Wales up to modern time in the folk prayer *Breuddwyd Mair*.[47]

Dafydd's poem goes on to list the Virgin's seven heavenly joys, a theme distinct from that of her five or seven earthly joys:

weithian o lan lywenydd
jddi saith gan dduw y sydd
vn yw kael gradd ai haddef
yn vwch noc engylion nef
ail vn bod i golevni
yn nef val yr haul ini
trydydd bod pob llywydd lles
vry yni henwin vrenhines
pedwerydd i rydd roddi
duw hael sydd vnvryd a hi
pymed hyn a geisied hon
duw ai gosyd yw gweision
chweched yw i byw ai bod
dryw vnder gar llawr drindod
seithved pvred y pery
j nwyf a roed i nef vry
archwn i vam grist erchi
er hyn oll ar hoi i ni
gael llewych golav llawen
gwledd i mab arglwydd amen[48]

Now she has seven pure joys from God. One is her receiving
a rank and dwelling higher than the angels of heaven; the
second, that her radiance in heaven is like the sun to us; the
third, that every beneficent ruler above names her as queen;
the fourth, that in bounteous giving the generous Lord's
thought is one with hers; the fifth, that whatever she asks for,
God gives it to her servants; the sixth is her living and
dwelling in unity with the Trinity; the seventh, how purely
lasts the joy given to heaven above. For the sake of all this we
beseech Christ's mother to ask that we be granted a gleam of
the joyful light at the feast of her Son, the Lord, Amen.

Dafydd's source for the above passage (as already
argued) is the Latin poem on the seven heavenly joys
beginning 'Gaude Virgo Laus Cunctorum', the work of
Christan von Lilienfeld (d. before 1332), prior of the
Austrian abbey of Lilienfeld, near St Polten, some thirty
miles west of Vienna. (The many manuscripts belonging
to Christan were still at Lilienfeld in the early twentieth
century, a comment on the seclusion of this Cistercian
house.) Although Christan's hymns did not circulate

widely in his lifetime, they influenced the work of a better-known Austrian writer, the Carthusian poet Konrad von Haimburg. The hymn below enjoyed a more vicarious influence via Ulrich Stöcklin von Rottach (d. 1443), abbot of the monastery of Wessobrunn, some forty miles south-west of Munich, near the Ammersee. Christan's hymn, which also exists in a Middle High German version, was attributed to Stöcklin for several centuries, and its true authorship was recognized only with the publication of *Analecta Hymnica.*

Gaude, virgo, laus cunctorum,   Gaude, tibi obsequentes
Super decus angelorum   Terrae et caeli gaudentes
  Tua fulget gloria;   Sument per te praemia
Gaude, dies ut ornatur   Gaude, angelis praelata
Sole, ita iucundatur   Trinitate proximata
  Caeli in te curia   Singulari gratia.

Gaude, te adorant caeli   Gaude, honor tuus crescit
Cives affectu fideli   Semper, quia finem nescit
  Et oboedientia;   Nec hic nec in patria;
Gaude, tuae voluntati   Gaude, virgo, mater Dei,
Affectus est trinitati   Nos duc reformatos ei
  Favere per omnia.   Ad festa caelestia.[49]

Be glad, O Virgin, the praise of others, because your glory outshines the glory of the angels. Be glad, because as the day is crowned by the sun, so the court of heaven is made joyful by you. Be glad, because the citizens of heaven adore you in faith and obedience. Be glad, because the Trinity is moved by your will to give help in all things. Be glad, because those who invoke you on earth and those who rejoice in heaven are rewarded through you. Be glad, queen of angels, because by unique grace you are placed next to the Trinity. Be glad, because your praise grows perpetually, knowing no end, either or in heaven. Be glad, O Virgin, mother of God, and lead us purified to him at heaven's banquets.

That this was Dafydd ab Edmwnd's source is seemingly proved by comparison of the closing lines with Dafydd's 'We beseech Christ's mother to ask that we be granted a gleam of the joyful light at the feast of her Son', against Christan's 'Be glad, O Virgin, mother of God, and lead us purified to him at heaven's banquets', where *gwledd i mab arglwydd* translates *festa caelestia*.

It is curious that Dafydd should have used *Gaude Virgo* as his source, and not the more popular *Gaude Flore Virginali*, especially as the first is unknown in Middle English verse, while we have several English translations of the second. But Dafydd's choice may be a tribute to his discernment. *Gaude Flore* is a wordy poem, and this feature is often made worse in translation. Comparison of the Welsh poem with those on this subject in Latin and English brings out Dafydd's (and Christan's) directness and clarity, qualities rare in much fifteenth-century English verse. However, Dafydd resembles the English poets of his time in his freedom as translator. The English 'To whom obeith as right quene / The court of heaven on hyghe' for *Cuius pendens est ad nutum / Tota celi curia* can thus be put beside Dafydd's *pob llywydd lles / vry yni henwin vrenhines* for *te adorant caeli / Cives affectu fideli*. The young Dafydd no doubt found this freedom useful as he worked on his prize poem through the night, in Carmarthen.

When we turn from Wales to Ireland, we find a poem on the Virgin's five sorrows in a tradition similar to (though not identical with) that of Dafydd ab Edmwnd's verses and the Thornton Manuscript prayer. The problem of the Irish poem is its date. If the poem is by the Donnchadh Mór Ó Dálaigh writing about 1400, it fits neatly with other passages on the five sorrows in English, Latin, and Welsh; but if it is by the Donnchadh Mór Ó Dálaigh who died in 1244, it predates these texts by well over a century.

The problem of the date of the Irish poem stands out sharply when set against the history of the devotion to the five sorrows as summed up by Dom Émile Bertraud.[50] According to Bertraud (and Wilmart), the tradition of the Virgin's five sorrows must derive from that of her five joys; but the five sorrows were apparently displaced fairly rapidly by the seven sorrows (first attested in Paris, BN, MS lat. 10527, an Avignon manuscript of about 1350 containing material predating the death of Pope John XXII in 1334), so that the only actual direct evidence for the five sorrows comes from a few late examples, none earlier that the late fourteenth century.

If the Irish poem really is by the earlier Donnchadh, it would be a precious find; unique evidence for the five sorrows in the earlier thirteenth century. But even without the facts cited above, his authorship would be dubious. Of the twenty-four poems in *Dioghluim Dána* which are attributed to the elder Donnchadh, McKenna remarks (p. 624) that, apart from number 29, we cannot be sure Donnchadh Mór wrote any of them. This blanket caveat, with all the other evidence from the late fourteenth century referred to above, makes attribution to the earlier Donnchadh most unlikely.

One wonders if Donnchadh's poem is a translation of a Latin hymn. If it were, it would take its place with other texts in *Dioghluim Dána* (numbers 15, 18, 19) that are translations from Latin (the Creed, the *Ave Maria*). But although Donnchadh's poem shares the same sequence of sorrows as do certain Latin hymns, it cannot be a translation of those on this subject in *Analecta Hymnica*:

> Cúig cáis as mhó le Moire
> dar fhuiling rí an ríoghthoighe
> tiocfa tráth as tuar toirse
> gidh fuar cách sna cásaibh-se.
> Fios báis a haoinmhic don óigh
> mar thair tarngaire Simóin
> fiu a dhoilghe do bhí fan mbás;
> ní ní gan chuimhne an chéadchás.
> An dara cás — cruaidh an sdair —
> sé ar seachrán re trí tráthaibh
> mar mhnaoi bhuile do bhí sain
> Muire agus í dá iarraidh.
> An treas cás do imthigh air
> — a fhios mar fhuair a mháthair
> gné do athruigh dá haghaidh —
> gabhthair é le híobhalaibh.
> Ar bhfaicsin Críost i gcruth bháis,

a ógh, ba adhbhar uathbháis
t'oidhre dod chomhair san chrann
go ngonaibh doimhne dearnann.
An ceathramhadh cás —'s é sain
shaorfas mé ar phéin an pheacaidh —
tre n-a croidhe do-chuaidh sin
Muire san uaigh dá fhaicsin.
Go raibh Muire uair m'éigne
ort, a Chríost, dar gcoimhéid-ne
's na cúig cáis ag labhra leam
's gach páis dá dtarla id thimcheall.
An ga do cuireadh id chíogh
le ceilg, a oidhre an airdríogh,
cuir led ghrásaibh lesi an nga
luibh leis na cásaibh céadna.[51]

A day will come when the five greatest sorrows of Mary that the King of Heaven suffered are a sign of grief, though each man is indifferent to them.

When the Virgin had foreknowledge from Simeon's prophecy of her only son's death, her affliction was no less than when her son died; the first sorrow is not forgotten.

The second sorrow, a harsh story, he being lost for three days, she was like a mad woman looking for him.

The third sorrow that occurred to him was arrest by the Jews; when his mother learned of it, her countenance changed.

It was cause for horror when you saw Christ on the point of dying, O Virgin, your son before you on the Cross, with deep wounds in his hands.

The fourth sorrow will free me from the penalty of sin: Mary's seeing her son in the grave, it pierced her heart.

May Mary when I sin against you protect me in my hour of need, O Lord, her five sorrows speaking on my behalf, and every grief she suffered through you.

The spear treacherously thrust in your side, Son of the High King, grant your grace with it, grant us a remedy with these sorrows.

From the material above we see that the devotion there to the Blessed Virgin's joys and sorrows accords with Continental forms of such devotions, while presenting features unknown in Middle English poetry. In short, the poems of Rhisierdyn, Dafydd ab Edmwnd, and Donnchadh Mór are not only strongly Celtic, but strongly European as well; like so much in medieval Welsh and Irish poetry, not only religious lyric, but love lyric and even political verse, which have never received full scholarly attention, and which remain a rich harvest that still awaits its gatherers.

As an example of what can be found, let us close this chapter and this book with a passage from *Gwr wyf, nid rhaid gwarafun*, an unpublished praise poem to the Virgin Mary by the Raglan bard Hywel ap Dafydd ab Ieuan ap Rhys (active about 1450–80).

Bepai'r ddaear yn bapir,
Pob pen fal dalen o dir,
Bai naf bob adaf bedydd,
A'r gwellt yn binnau a'r gwŷdd,
Merch ewybr, morach ieuainc,
Morwyn yw, a'r môr yn ainc,
A'r coed a'r rhedyn a'r cyll,
Ban osgl yn binnau esgyll
Yn llwyr, a phob pin yn llaw
Union deitl yn endeitiaw,
Ni ellid uwchben allawr
Adrodd ei gwyrth, deurudd gwawr,
Na'i moddion teg, meddiant dwys,
Na'i phryd, mwy no pharadwys.[52]

If the earth were paper, every part like a page of earth, if every Christian hand held sway and the grass and the trees pens (resplendent maiden, the young people's joy, virgin is she), and the sea ink, and the trees and ferns and hazels quill pens, high-branched, and every pen in hand inditing a fit title: her miracle above the altar could not be told, cheeks of dawn, nor her fair ways, solemn power, nor her beauty more than paradise.

This variant of Ernst Curtius's 'inexpressibility topos' is the one parodied in the well-known nursery rhyme, found as early as Charles I's reign:

> If all the world were paper,
> And all the sea were ink,
> If all the trees were bread and cheese,
> What should we have to drink?

The theme is in fact a very ancient and widespread one. It first appears in Sanskrit, and then becomes a feature of Jewish commentary and devotional writing. A phrase from the Talmud is typical of these early examples, saying that if all seas were ink and all rushes pens and the whole Heaven parchment and all sons of men writers, they would not be enough to describe the depth of the mind of the Lord. The nursery rhyme above has been called a parody of the use of such extravagant phrases in Jewish devotion. It seems almost certain that the theme reached Wales from India through the influence of the Jews in medieval Europe.[53]

The earliest use of the theme in European literature seems to be in a poem by Marbod of Rennes (*c.*1035–1123), though the attribution has been doubted.

> Si fiat calamus stans omnis in arbore ramus,
> Fiat et incaustrum, quod suggerit omnibus haustum,
> Si pro membrana sint omnia corpora plana,
> Vivi vel functi si scribant talia cuncti,
> Vivos vel functos lassabunt talia cunctos.[54]

It certainly appears, however, in the *Elegia* of Henricus of Settimello, written in Italy in 1191 or 1192.

> Pagina sit celum, sint frondes scribe, sit unda
> Incaustum: mala non nostra referre queant.[55]

In the *Doligamus* of Adolf of Vienna, writing about 1315, the theme has been given the anti-feminist twist which it long retained.

Si stelle scribe, pelles celum, maris unda
Esset incaustum, nec ciffra cum sociis
Sufficerent plene mulierum scribere fraudes,
Cum quibus illaqueant corda modo iuvenum.[56]

Similar sentiments appear in the thirteenth-century *Lamentations* of Matheolus, a screed of anti-feminist tales translated from Latin into French in the fourteenth century, which enjoyed long popularity thereafter.[57]

The theme is in fact a commonplace of medieval literature, and Köhler was able to quote instances from Johann von Freiberg's *Das Rädlein*, Reinbot von Dürn's poem to St George, and the Castilian translation *Libro de los engannos et los asayamientos de las mugeres*, all of them dating from the thirteenth century, as well as from Old French courtly and religious poetry. In the modern period evidence for the theme becomes abundant, and examples have been found in folk-songs from Greece, Turkey, Hungary, Spain, Venezuela, and many other countries. This diffusion of the theme of the sky or world as paper is strikingly like that of the international popular tales described by Kenneth Jackson, so many of which may be followed over a period of a thousand or more years from ancient Indian sources via Jewish or Near Eastern texts to dozens of modern European languages and even the New World.[58]

The first appearance in English of the topos is in the anti-feminist poem 'Loke well about, ye that louers be', attributed to John Lydgate (*c.*1370–1452).

In soothe to say, though all the erthe so wanne
  Were parchemine smoothe, white, and scribàble;
And the gret see that called is the ociànne
  Were turnèd into inke blakker than sable;
Every stik a penne, eche man a scrivener able:
  Not coude they then write womans trechery.
  Be ware therfore — the blinde eteth many a fly.[59]

Closer in spirit to Hywel ap Dafydd's verses is another fifteenth-century poem to the Virgin, 'Cloister of Christ, riche recent flour-de-lyss', by the Middle Scots poet Walter

Kennedy (*c*.1460–*c*.1508). It contains this stanza:

> The moder' se / fludis / lochis / and wellis
> War' all thir' ynke & quyk & deid couth wryte
> The hevyne stellat montanis planetis & fellis
> War' faire parchiament & all as virgillis dyte
> And plesand pennis for to report perfyte
> War woddis / forestis / treis / gardingis / & grawis
> Couth nocht discryve thi honouris Infinit
> *Speciosa facta es et suavis.*[60]

The theme appears elsewhere in the Scottish poetry of this period, as in the Bannatyne Manuscript, though usually for anti-feminist satire.[61] In this guise it reached Ireland, as has been shown in discussion of an epigram from a seventeenth-century manuscript.[62] It is, therefore, of interest that this ancient oriental figure, having long entered the Latin learning of medieval Europe and the vernaculars of France, Spain, and Germany, should appear at about the same time in the poetry of late medieval England, Wales, and Scotland; and that it should there naturally be applied to praise of the Virgin.

Even a book of this length must close with the sense that a mere fraction of what might be presented has been brought forward; and that what survives from the Middle Ages is a million-millionth of that love of the Virgin which was then a matter of thought and meditation and prayer. So, after quoting so many Irish and Welsh poets, we may end with an English one, the scholar Alcuin (d. 804), who here spoke in few words but well-chosen, saying 'Virgin Mary, mother of God, virgin most chaste, light and star of the sea, queen of our salvation':

> Virgo Maria dei genitrix, castissima virgo,
> Lux et stella maris, nostrae regina salutis.[63]

Notes

1. *Navarre Bible: St Luke's Gospel*, p. 44.
2. Breeze, 'Master John of St Davids, a New Twelfth-Century Poet?', 73–82
3. R. T. Davies, p. 376; Casagrande, p. 165.
4. Trens, pp. 296–9; Gray, p. 89; Greene, p. 116.
5. Reiners, p. 919.
6. Greene, p. 126.
7. Dreves and Blume, i, pp. 130, 216.
8. Santob de Carrión, p. 70; G. A. Davies, p. 22.
9. Dreves and Blume, i, p. 269.
10. Haycock, p. 354.
11. Hümer, p. 46; Casagrande, p. 867.
12. Cf. Cahill.
13. Neil Wright, pp. 61–76.
14. Colgrave and Mynors, p. 514; Aldhelm, pp. 13–14.
15. Stevenson p. 163; Aldhelm, pp. 1, 179.
16. Levison, pp. 133–4; Wormald, Patrick, p. 90.
17. Parkes, p. 151; Sims-Williams, p. 359, n. 129.
18. Levison, pp. 161–2. Just as Noah escaped the Flood, so this one manuscript escaped the destruction of all others in the library. (Somebody must have borrowed it.) Cassiodorus was an early Christian monk; his book on the duties of monks helped in the formation of the Benedictine Order.
19. Stevenson, pp. 162–3; Lapidge and Keynes, pp. 53–4.
20. Jackson, *Language*, p. 62.
21. Ibid., pp. 50–1; Ker, p. 418; Bishop, p. 19; Oates, 81–7.
22. Stevenson, pp. 163; Whitelock, pp. 911–12.
23. Francis Wormald, p. 27; L. J. Lloyd, p. 36.
24. Dronke, p. 552; Rigg and Wieland, pp. 113–30.
25. Stevenson, pp. 163.
26. Barlow, p. 242.
27. Wilson, p. 98; Ogilvy, pp. 239–40; Gneuss, 1–60.
28. Curtius, p. 460.
29. Dronke, pp. 181–92.
30. Barré, 'Sermons marials', 89–90; Hamman, cols 1989–90.
31. Dreves and Blume, ii, p. 267; Szövérffy, i. pp. 341–3.
32. Southern, *St Anselm*, p. 289; Woolf, *English Religious Lyric*, pp. 134–6.
33. Salu, pp. 15–17, 195–6; cf. Robertson, pp. 131–2.
34. Brown, *English Lyrics of the Thirteenth Century*, pp. 27–9, 32–3, 65–7.
35. Gwenogvryn Evans, col. 1251.
36. Woolf, *English Religious Lyric*, pp. 138, 141; Breeze, 'Blessed Virgin's Joys', 44.

37. Bowen, pp. 82–3.
38. John Jones and Walter Davies, p. 126; cf. Johnston, *Gwaith Lewys Glyn Cothi*.
39. John Jones and Walter Davies, p. 415.
40. E. Stanton Roberts, p. 76.
41. Bachellery, i, p. 147.
42. Thomas Roberts of Bangor, p. 164; cf. Nesta Lloyd, 120–4.
43. Ifor Williams and Thomas Roberts, p. 184.
44. Thomas Roberts of Bangor, pp. 123–4.
45. Wilmart, pp. 508, n. 8, 513, n. 4.
46. Horstmann, i, p. 378.
47. Glanmor Williams, p. 480.
48. Thomas Roberts, p. 123.
49. Dreves and Blume, i, p. 412.
50. Bertaud, cols 1692–3.
51. McKenna, *Dioghluim*, p. 46; cf. O'Dwyer, *Mary*, pp. 86–7.
52. Breeze, 'Bepai'r ddaear yn bapir', 274.
53. Opie and Opie, p. 436–8; cf. Singer, p. 367.
54. Breeze, 'Bepai'r ddaear yn bapir', 275.
55. It is item 20567 in Walther.
56. It is item 29189 in Walther.
57. It is item 28493 in Walther.
58. Jackson, *International Popular Tale*, pp. 7–8, 12–13, 20, 22, 39–40, 45–6.
59. Sisam and Sisam, p. 566.
60. Craigie, ii, pp. 272–5.
61. Ritchie, ii, p. 258, iii, pp. 23, 73.
62. Mac Mathúna, pp. 121–2.
63. Howse, p. 115.

Bibliography

Adnès, Pierre, 'Larmes', in *Dictionnaire de Spiritualité*, ix (Paris, Beauchesne, 1976), cols 287–303.

Aldhelm, *The Prose Works* (Ipswich, Brewer, 1979).

Alfonso X, *Cantigas de Santa María* (Madrid, Castalia, 1985).

Algermissen, Konrad and Böer, Ludwig (eds), *Lexikon der Marienkunde* (Regensburg, Pistet, 1967).

Anderson, Marjorie, *Kings and Kingship in Early Scotland* (Edinburgh, Scottish Academic Press, 1973).

Anker, Peter, *L'art scandinave* (Paris, Zodiaque, 1968).

Ashton, Charles (ed.), *Gweithiau Iolo Goch* (Croesoswallt, Cymmrodorion, 1898).

Bachellery, E. (ed.), *L'Oeuvre poétique de Gutun Owain* (Paris, Champion, 1950–1).

Banning, Knud, *A Catalogue of Wall-Paintings in the Churches of Medieval Denmark 1100–1600* (Copenhagen, Akademisk, 1976–82).

Barlow, Frank, Dexter, Kathleen, Erskine, Audrey and Lloyd, L. J., 'Leofric and his Times', in Frank Barlow et al., *Leofric of Exeter* (Exeter, University of Exeter, 1972), 1–16.

—— *The English Church 1066–1154* (London, Longman, 1979).

Barré, Henri, 'Le ""mystère" d'Ève à la fin de l'époque patristique en Occident', *Bulletin de la société française des études mariales*, xiii (1955), 61–97.

—— 'Le sermon "Exhortatur" est-il de Saint Ildefonse?',

Revue bénédictine, lxvii (1957), 10–33.

—— *Les homéliaires carolingiens de l'école d'Auxerre* (Città del Vaticano, Biblioteca Apostolica, 1962).

—— 'Sermons marials inédits "in Natali Domini"', *Marianum*, xxv (1963), 39–93.

Baumer, Christoph, 'Die Schreinmadonna', *Marian Library Studies*, ix (1977), 237–72.

Bäumer, Remigius and Scheffczyk, Leo (eds), *Marienlexikon* (St Ottilien, Eos, 1988–94).

Beadle, Richard (ed.), *The York Plays* (London, Arnold, 1982).

Becker, Heinrich, *Die Auffassung der Jungfrau Maria in der altfranzösischen Litteratur* (Göttingen, Universitäts Buchdrukerei, 1905).

Beissel, Stephen, *Geschichte der Verehrung Marias in Deutschland wärend des Mittelalters* (Freiburg im Breisgau, Herder, 1909).

Bennett, H. S., *Life on the English Manor* (Cambridge, Cambridge University Press, 1937).

Bennett, J. A. W., and Gray, Douglas, *Middle English Literature* (Oxford, Clarendon, 1986).

Bennett, J. A. W. and Smithers, G. V. (eds), *Early Middle English Verse and Prose*, 2nd edn (Oxford, Clarendon, 1968).

Benson, Larry D. (ed.), *The Riverside Chaucer* (Oxford, Oxford University Press, 1988).

Berger, Pamela, *Transformation of the Grain Protectress from Goddess to Saint* (Boston, Beacon, 1985).

Bergin, Osborn, Greene, David and Kelly, Fergus (eds), *Irish Bardic Poetry* (Dublin, DIAS, 1970).

Bertaud, Émile, 'Notre-Dame des Sept-Douleurs', *Dictionnaire de Spiritualité*, iii (Paris, Beauchesne, 1957), cols 1692–3.

Bischoff, Bernhard, 'Turning-Points in the History of Latin Exegesis', in *Biblical Studies: The Medieval Irish Contribution*, ed. Martin McNamara (Dublin, Dominican Publications, 1975), 73–160.

Bishop, T. A. M., *English Caroline Minuscule* (Oxford, Clarendon, 1971).

Blake, N. F., *The English Language in Medieval Literature* (London, Dent, 1977).

Bliss, Alan, and Long, Joseph, 'Literature in Norman French and English to 1534', in *A New History of Ireland: Medieval Ireland*, ed. Art Cosgrove (Oxford, Clarendon, 1987), 708–36.

Bock, Franz, *Der Reliquienschatz des Liebfrauen-Münsters zu Aachen* (Aachen, privately printed, 1860).

Borenius, Tancred and Tristram, E. W., *English Medieval Painting* (Florence, Pantheon, 1927).

Borsook, Eve, *The Mural Painters of Tuscany*, 2nd edn (Oxford, Clarendon, 1980).

Boss, Sarah, *Empress and Handmaid* (London, Cassell, 2000).

Bowen, D. J. (ed.), *Barddoniaeth yr Uchelwyr* (Cardiff, Gwasg Prifysgol Cymru, 1957).

Brandon, S. G. F., *Man and His Destiny in the Great Religions* (Manchester, Manchester University Press, 1962).

Brasas Egido, J. C., *La platería palentina* (Palencia, Diputación Provincial, 1982).

Breeze, Andrew, 'Bepai'r ddaear yn bapir', *Bulletin of the Board of Celtic Studies*, xxx (1982–83), 274–74.

—— 'The Number of Christ's Wounds', *Bulletin of the Board of Celtic Studies*, xxxii (1985), 84–91.

—— 'Madog ap Gwallter', *Ysgrifau Beirniadol*, xiii (1985), 93–9.

—— 'The Girdle of Prato and its Rivals', *Bulletin of the Board of Celtic Studies*, xxxiii (1986), 95–100.

—— 'Postscripta', *Bulletin of the Board of Celtic Studies*, xxxv (1988), 50–1.

—— 'The Virgin's Tears of Blood', *Celtica*, xx (1988), 110–22.

—— 'The Virgin's Rosary and St Michael's Scales', *Studia Celtica*, xxiv-xxv (1989–90), 91–8.

—— 'The Blessed Virgin's Joys and Sorrows', *Cambridge Medieval Cambridge Studies*, xix (1990), 41–54.

—— 'The Instantaneous Harvest', *Ériu*, xli (1990), 81–93.

—— 'Job's Gold in Medieval England, Wales, and Navarre', *Notes and Queries*, ccxxxv (1990), 275–8.

—— 'Two Bardic Themes: The Trinity in the Blessed Virgin's Womb, and the Rain of Folly', *Celtica*, xxii (1991), 1–15.

—— '*Beowulf* 875–902 and the Sculptures at Sangüesa, Spain', *Notes and Queries*, ccxxxvi (1991), 2–13.

—— 'The Virgin Mary and Romance', *SELIM*, i (1991), 144–51.

—— 'The Instantaneous Harvest and the Harley Lyric *Mayden Moder Milde*', *Notes and Queries*, ccxxxvii (1992), 150–2.

—— 'Master John of St Davids, a New Twelfth-Century Poet?', *Bulletin of the Board of Celtic Studies*, xl (1993), 73–82.

—— 'The Virgin Mary and *The Dream of the Rood*', *Florilegium*, xii (1993), 55–62.

—— 'Welsh *Cais* "Sergeant" and *Sawles Warde*', *Notes and Queries*, ccxxxviii (1993), 297–303.

—— 'Two Bardic Themes: the Virgin and Child, and *Ave-Eva*', *Medium Aevum*, lxiii (1994), 17–33.

—— 'Master John of St Davids, Adam and Eve, and the Rose amongst Thorns', *Studia Celtica*, xxix (1995), 225–35.

—— *Medieval Welsh Literature* (Dublin, 1997).

—— 'The Virgin Mary, Daughter of her Son', *Études celtiques*, xxvii (1990), 267–83.

—— 'The Blessed Virgin and the Sunbeam through Glass', *Celtica*, xxiii (1999), 19–29.

—— 'The Date of the Ruthwell Cross Inscription', *American Notes and Queries* xvi/2 (2003), 3–5.

Bridgett, T. E., *Our Lady's Dowry*, 3rd edn (London, Burns & Oates, 1894).

Broby-Johansen, R., *Den Danske Billedbibel* ([Copenhagen,] Gyldendal, 1947).

Bromwich, Rachel and Evans, D. Simon (eds), *Culhwch and Olwen* (Cardiff, University of Wales Press, 1992).

Brook, G. L. (ed.), *The Harley Lyrics* (Manchester, Manchester University Press, 1948).

Brown, Carleton (ed.), *English Lyrics of the XIIIth Century* (Oxford, Clarendon, 1932).

—— (ed.), *Religious Lyrics of the XVth Century* (Oxford, Clarendon, 1939).

— (ed.), *Religious Lyrics of the XIVth Century*, 2nd edn (Oxford, Clarendon, 1952).

Burlin, R. B. (ed.), *The Old English Advent* (New Haven, Yale University Press, 1968).

Byrne, F. J., *Irish Kings and High-Kings* (London, Batsford, 1973).

Cahill, Michael (ed.), *The First Commentary on Mark* (New York, Oxford University Press, 1998).

Caiger-Smith, Alan, *English Medieval Mural Paintings* (Oxford, Clarendon, 1963).

Carney, James (ed.), *Poems of Blathmac* (Dublin, ITS, 1964).

Cartwright, Jane, *Y Forwyn Fair, Santesau, a Lleianod* (Cardiff, Gwasg Prifysgol Cymru, 1999).

Casagrande, Domenico (ed.), *Enchiridion Marianum Biblicum Patristicum* (Rome, Cor Unum, 1974).

Cave, C. J. P., *Roof Bosses in Medieval Churches* (Cambridge, Cambridge University Press, 1948).

Chadwick, Nora, *The Age of the Saints in the Early Celtic Church* (London, Oxford University Press, 1961).

Chambers, E. K. and Sidgwick, Frank (eds), *Early English Lyrics* (London, Sidgwick and Jackson, 1907).

Chapman, Reginald, *Saint Botolph's Church, Slapton* (Towcester, privately printed, 1976).

Cheetham, Francis, *English Medieval Alabasters* (Oxford, Phaidon, 1984).

Christie, A. G. I., *English Medieval Embroidery* (Oxford, Clarendon, 1938).

Christmas, Henry (ed.), *Select Works of John Bale* (Cambridge, Cambridge University Press, 1849).

Cignelli, Lino, *Maria Nuova Eva nella Patristica greca* (Assisi, Porziuncola, 1966).

Clancy, J. P., *Medieval Welsh Lyrics* (London, Macmillan, 1965).

—— *The Earliest Welsh Poetry* (London, Macmillan, 1970).

Clancy, T. O. and Márkus, Gilbert, *Iona: The Earliest Poetry of a Celtic Monastery* (Edinburgh, Edinburgh University Press, 1995).

Clayton, Mary, *The Cult of the Virgin Mary in Anglo-Saxon England* (Cambridge, Cambridge University Press, 1990).

Coates, Richard and Breeze, Andrew, *Celtic Voices, English Places* (Stamford, Shaun Tyas, 2000).

Colgrave, Bertram and Mynors, R. A. B. (eds), *Bede's Ecclesiastical History* (Oxford, Clarendon, 1969).

Contini, Gianfranco (ed.), *Poeti del Duecento* (Milan, Ricciardi, 1960).

Cowley, F. G., *The Monastic Order in South Wales 1066–1349* (Cardiff, University of Wales Press, 1977).

Craigie, W. A. (ed.), *The Asloan Manuscript* (Edinburgh, Blackwood, 1923–5).

Curtius, E. R., *European Literature and the Latin Middle Ages* (New York, Pantheon, 1953).

Cynddelw (ed.), *Gorchestion Beirdd Cymru* (Caernarfon, Humphreys, 1864).

Dagens, Jean, 'La métaphore de la verrière', *Revue d'Ascétique et de mystique*, xxv (1949), 524–32.

Davies, G. A., *Y Ffynnon sy'n Ffrydio* (Caerdydd, Gwasg Prifysgol Cymru, 1990).

Davies, Oliver, *Celtic Christianity in Early Medieval Wales* (Cardiff, University of Wales Press, 1996).

Davies, R. R., *Wales 1063–1415* (Oxford, Clarendon, 1987).

Davies, R. T. (ed.), *Medieval English Lyrics* (London, Faber, 1963).

de Aldama, J. A., *Repertorium Pseudochrysostomicum* (Paris, CNRS, 1965).

de Brun, Pádraig, Ó Buachalla, Breandán and Ó Concheanainn, Tomás (eds), *Nua-dhuanaire*, i (Baile átha Cliath, Dublin, DIAS, 1975).

Deschamps, Paul, and Thibout, Marc, *La peinture murale en France au début de l'époque gothique* (Paris, CNRS, 1963).

Díaz y Díaz, M. C., 'J. Madoz, *Segundo decenario de estudios sobre Patrística Española*', *Revista española de teología*, xii (1952), 278–83.

—— (ed.), *Liber de Ordine Creaturarum* (Santiago de Compostela, University of Santiago, 1972).

Dictionary of the Irish Language (Dublin, RIA, 1913–76).

The Dictionary of Welsh Biography (London, Cymmrodorion, 1959).

Dobson, E. J., *The Origins of 'Ancrene Wisse'* (Oxford, Clarendon, 1976).

Dobson, E. J. and Harrison, F. Ll. (eds), *Medieval English Songs* (London, Faber, 1979).

Dreves, G. M. and Blume, Clemens (eds), *Ein Jahrtausend Lateinischer Hymnendichtung* (Leipzig, Reizland, 1909).

Dronke, Peter, *Medieval Latin and the Rise of European Love-Lyric*, 2nd edn (Oxford, Clarendon, 1968).

Dumville, D. N., 'Biblical Apocrypha and the Early Irish', *Proceedings of the Royal Irish Academy*, lxxiii C (1973), 299–338.

Las Edades del Hombre: Libros y Documentos en la Iglesia de Castilla y León (Burgos, Diócesis de Castilla y León, 1990).

Edwards, John, 'A "Fifteenth-Century" Wall-Painting at South Leigh', *Oxoniensia*, xlviii (1983), 131–42.

—— 'The Medieval Wall-Paintings Formerly at St Andrew's Church, Headington, Oxford', *Archaeological Journal*, cxlv (1988), 263–71.

Erbe, Theodor (ed.), *Mirk's Festial*, EETS e.s. 96 (London, Kegan Paul, 1905).

Estella, Margarita, *La escultura del marfil en España* (Madrid, Nacional, 1984), 125–46.

Evans, D. F. (ed.), *Gwaith Hywel Swrdwal a'i Deulu* (Aberystwyth, Canolfan Uwchefrydiau, 2000).

Evans, D. Simon, *Writers of Wales: Medieval Religious Literature* (Cardiff, University of Wales Press, 1986).

Evans, J. Gwenogvryn (ed.), *The Poetry in the Red Book of Hergest* (Llanbedrog, privately printed, 1911).

Farmer, D. H., 'The Studies of Anglo-Saxon Monks', in *Los monjes y los estudios* (Poblet, Abadía de Poblet, 1963), 87–103.

Flete, John, *The History of Westminster Abbey* (Cambridge, Cambridge University Press, 1909).

Flower, Robin, *The Irish Tradition* (Oxford, Clarendon, 1947).

Folz, Robert, *Le Souvenir et la légende de Charlemagne* (Paris, University of Dijon, 1950).

Foster, Frances (ed.), *The Northern Passion*, EETS o.s. 145 (London, Kegan Paul, 1913).

Gębarowicz, Mieczyslaw, *Mater Misericordiae* (Wroclaw, Ossolinksi, 1986).

Gneuss, Helmut, 'Latin Hymns in Medieval England', in *Chaucer and Middle English Studies*, ed. Beryl Rowland (London, Unwin, 1974), 407–24.

—— 'A Preliminary List of Manuscripts Written or Owned in England up to 1100', *Anglo-Saxon England*, xi (1981), 1–60.

Godden, Malcolm (ed.), *Ælfric's Catholic Homilies*, EETS s.s. 5 (Oxford, Oxford University Press, 1979).

Gonzalo de Berceo, *Obras completas*, iii (London, Támesis, 1975).

Gould, Karen (ed.), *The Psalter and Hours of Yolande of Soissons* (Cambridge, Mass., Medieval Academy of America, 1978).

Graef, Hilda, *Mary: A History of Doctrine and Devotion* (London, Sheed and Ward, 1963–5).

Gray, Douglas, *Themes and Images in the Medieval English Religious Lyric* (London, RKP, 1972).

—— (ed.), *A Selection of Religious Lyrics* (Oxford, Clarendon, 1975).

Gray, Madeleine and Ryan, Salvador, 'Mother of Mercy: The Virgin Mary and the Last Judgement in Welsh and Irish Tradition', in /Ireland and Wales in the Middle Ages/, ed. Karen Jankulak and Jonathan M. Wooding (Dublin, Four Courts, 2007), 246–61.

Greene, R. L. (ed.), *The Early English Carols*, 2nd edn (Oxford, Clarendon, 1977).

Harris, Markham (tr.), *The Cornish Ordinalia* (Washington, Catholic University of America, 1969).

Hamman, Adalbert (ed.), *Patrologiae Cursus Completus, series latina: Supplementum* (Paris, Garnier, 1958–75).

Haycock, Marged (ed.), *Blodeugerdd Barddas o Ganu Crefyddol Cynnar* (n.p., Bardas, 1994).

Herbert, Máire, *Iona, Kells, and Derry* (Oxford, Clarendon, 1988).

Herrán, L. M., *Mariología poética española* (Madrid, BAC, 1988).

Hildburgh, W. L., 'An English Alabaster Carving of St Michael Weighing a Soul', *Burlington Magazine*, lxxxix (1947), 129–31.

Hirn, Yrjö, *The Sacred Shrine* (London, Faber, 1958).

Horgan, A. D., 'The Dream of the Rood and Christian Tradition', *Neuphilologische Mitteilungen*, lxxix (1978), 11–20.

Horstmann, Carl (ed.), *Yorkshire Writers* (London, Sonnenschein, 1895).

Horstmann, Carl and Furnivall, F. J., *The Minor Poems of the Vernon MS*, EETS o.s. 98, 117 (London, Kegan Paul, 1892–1901).

Howse, Christopher (ed.), *Prayers for this Life* (London, Continuum, 2005).

Hueser, Wilhelm (ed.), *Die Kildare-Gedichte* (Bonn, Hanstein, 1904).

Hughes, Kathleen, *The Church in Early Irish Society* (London, Methuen, 1966).

Huizinga, Johan, *Herbst des Mittelalters* (Stuttgart, Kröner, 1965).

—— *The Waning of the Middle Ages* (Harmondsworth, Penguin, 1972).

Hümer, Johann (ed.), *Seduli Opera Omnia* (Vienna, Vindobona, Geroldi, 1885).

Huon le Roi de Cambrai, *Oeuvres*, i (Paris, Champion, 1913).

Huppé, B. F., *The Web of Words* (Albany, SUNY, 1970).

Jackson, K. H., 'A Note on the Miracle of the Instantaneous Harvest', *Bulletin of the Board of Celtic Studies*, x (1939–41), 203–7.

—— 'Some Fresh Light on the Miracle of the Instantaneous Harvest', *Folklore*, li (1940), 203–10.

—— *Language and History in Early Britain* (Edinburgh, Edinburgh University Press, 1953).

—— *The International Popular Tale and Early Welsh Tradition* (Cardiff, University of Wales Press, 1961).

—— *A Celtic Miscellany*, 2nd edn (Harmondsworth, Penguin, 1971).

James, M. R., *The Apocryphal New Testament* (Oxford, Clarendon, 1924).

Johnston, D. R. (ed.), *Gwaith Iolo Goch* (Cardiff, Gwasg Prifysgol Cymru, 1988).

—— (ed.), *Blodeugerdd Barddas o'r Bedwaredd Ganrig ar Ddeg* (n.p., Bardas, 1989).

—— (ed.), *Gwaith Lewys Glyn Cothi* (Cardiff, Gwasg Prifysgol Cymru, 1995).

Jones, G. Hartwell, *Celtic Britain and the Pilgrim Movement* (London, Cymmrodorion, 1912).

Jones, Glyn Penrhyn, 'The Welsh Poet as a Medical Historian', in *Wales and Medicine*, ed. John Cule (n.p., British Society for the History of Medicine, 1975), 119–26.

Jones, Gwenan (ed.), *Three Welsh Religious Plays* (Bala, Bala Press, 1939).

Jones, H. Ll. and Rowlands, E. I. (ed.), *Gwaith Iorwerth Fynglwyd* (Cardiff, Gwasg Prifysgol Cymru, 1975).

Jones, John and Davies, Walter (eds), *Gwaith Lewis Glyn Cothi* (Oxford, Cymmrodorion, 1836–9).

Jones, Owen et al. (eds), *The Myvyrian Archaiology of Wales*, 2nd edn (Denbigh, Gee, 1870).

Jones, T. Gwynn (ed.), *Gwaith Tudur Aled* (Cardiff, Gwasg Prifysgol Cymru, 1926).

Juan Manuel, Infante don, *Libro de los Estados* (Oxford, Clarendon, 1974).

Kaftal, George, *Iconography of the Saints in Central and Southern Italian Painting* (Florence, Sansoni, 1965).

Kenney, J. F., *The Sources for the Early History of Ireland: Ecclesiastical* (New York, Columbia University Press, 1929).

Ker, N. R., *Catalogue of Manuscripts containing Anglo-Saxon* (Oxford, Clarendon, 1957).

—— *Medieval Manuscripts in British Libraries*, ii (Oxford, Clarendon, 1977).

—— (ed.), *Medieval Libraries of Great Britain*, 2nd edn (London, Royal Historical Society, 1964).

Kinkade, R. P. (ed.), *Los 'Lucidarios' españoles* (Madrid, Gredos, 1968).

Kirschbaum, Engelbert (ed.), *Lexikon der christlichen Ikonographie* (Rome, Herder, 1968–76).

Korhammer, P. M., 'The Origin of the Bosworth Psalter',

Anglo-Saxon England, ii (1973), 173–87.

Lapidge, Michael and Keynes, Simon, *Alfred the Great* (Harmondsworth, Penguin, 1983).

Lapidge, Michael and Sharpe, Richard, *A Bibliography of Celtic-Latin Literature 400–1200* (Dublin, RIA, 1985).

Legge, M. Dominica, *Anglo-Norman in the Cloisters* (Edinburgh, Edinburgh University Press, 1950).

Levison, Wilhelm, *England and the Continent in the Eighth Century* (Oxford, Clarendon, 1946).

Lewis, Henry (ed.), *Hen Gerddi Crefyddol* (Cardiff, Gwasg Prifysgol Cymru, 1931).

Lewis, Henry et al. (eds), *Cywyddau Iolo Goch ac Eraill*, 2nd edn (Cardiff, Gwasg Prifysgol Cymru, 1937).

Lipphardt, Walther, 'Studien zu den Marienklagen', *Beiträge zur Geschichte der deutschen Sprache und Literatur*, lviii (1934), 390–444.

Lizarralde, J. A., *Andra Mari* (Bilbao, Dochao, 1926).

Lloyd, D. Myrddin, *Rhai Agweddau ar Ddysg y Gogynfeirdd* (Cardiff, Gwasg Prifysgol Cymru, 1977).

Lloyd, L. J., 'Leofric as Bibliophile', in Frank Barlow et al., *Leofric of Exeter* (Exeter, University of Exeter, 1972), 32–42.

Lloyd, Nesta, 'Ystoria Pedair Morwyn y Drindod', *Bulletin of the Board of Celtic Studies*, xxv (1972–4), 120–4.

Lloyd-Jones, John, *Geirfa Barddoniaeth Gynnar Gymraeg* (Cardiff, Gwasg Prifysgol Cymru, 1931–63).

Longère, Jean, *La prédication médiévale* (Paris, Études augustieniennes, 1983).

Lowe, E. A., *Palaeographical Papers 1907–1965* (Oxford, Clarendon, 1972).

Lumby, J. R. and McKnight, G. H. (eds), *King Horn, Floris and Blauncheflur, The Assumption of Our Lady*, EETS o.s. 14 (London, Kegan Paul, 1901).

Lydgate, John, *Poems* (Oxford, Clarendon, 1966).

Mac Mathúna, Ciarán, 'Samhlaíocht a Thaisteal', *Éigse*, vii (1953), 121–2.

Madigan, Brian, 'Van Eyck's Illuminated Carafe', *Journal of the Warburg and Courtauld Institutes*, xlix (1986), 227–30.

Madoz, José, *Le Symbole du XIᵉ Concile de Tolède* (Louvain, Spicilegium, 1938).

Mâle, Émile, *L'Art religieux de XIIIième siècle en France* (Paris, Colin, 1925).

—— *The Gothic Image* (London, Fontana, 1961).

Mayer, Anton, 'Mater et Filia: ein Versuch zur stilgeschichtlichen Entwicklung eines Gebetsausdrucks', *Jahrbuch für Liturgiewissenschaft*, vii (1927), 60–82.

Mayr-Harting, H. M., *The Coming of Christianity to Anglo-Saxon England* (London, Batsford, 1972).

McNamara, Martin, *The Apocrypha in the Irish Church* (Dublin, DIAS, 1975).

—— 'Celtic Christianity, Creation and Apocalypse, Christ and Antichrist', *Milltown Studies*, xxiii (1989), 5–39.

Mac Craith, Mícheál, 'Literature in Irish, c.1550–1690', in *The Cambridge History of Irish Literature*, ed. Margaret Kelleher and Philip O'Leary (Cambridge, Cambridge University Press, 2006).

Mac Niocaill, Gearóid, 'Carta Humani Generis', *Éigse*, viii (1955–7), 204–21.

McKenna, Lambert (ed.), *Dánta do chum Aonghus Fionn ó Dálaigh* (Dublin, Maunsel, 1919).

—— (ed.), *Dán Dé* (Dublin, Educational Company of Ireland, 1922).

—— (ed.), *Philip Bocht O hUiginn* (Dublin, Talbot, 1931).

—— (ed.), *Dioghluim Dána* (Dublin, Oifig an tSoláthair, 1938).

—— (ed.), *Aithdioghluim Dána* (Dublin, ITS, 1939–40).

Meiss, Millard, 'Light as Form and Symbol in Some Fifteenth-Century Paintings', *Art Bulletin*, xxvii (1945), 175–81.

Migne, J.-P. (ed.), *Patrologia Graeca* (Paris, Garnier, 1857–1912).

Moore, Elsie, 'Wall-Paintings Recently Discovered in Worcestershire', *Archaeologia*, lxxxviii (1938), 281–8.

Murdoch, Brian, *Cornish Literature* (Cambridge, Brewer, 1993).

Murphy, Gerard, *Early Irish Metrics* (Dublin, RIA, 1961).

—— (ed.), *Early Irish Lyrics* (Oxford, Clarendon, 1956).

The Navarre Bible: St Luke's Gospel (Dublin, Four Courts, 1988).

Nelson, Philip, 'Some Unusual English Alabaster Panels', *Transactions of the Historic Society of Lancashire and Cheshire*, lxix (1917), 80–96.

—— 'Some Fifteenth-Century Alabaster Panels', *Archaeological Journal*, lxxvi (1919), 133–8.

Newton, P. A., *The County of Oxford: A Catalogue of Medieval Stained Glass* (London, Oxford University Press, 1979).

Oates, J. C. T., 'Notes on the Later History of the Oldest Manuscript of Welsh Poetry', *Cambridge Medieval Celtic Studies*, iii (1982), 81–7.

Obregón Barreda, Luis, *María en los Padres de la Iglesia* (Madrid, Ciudad Nueva, 1988).

Ó Caithnia, L. P., *Apalóga na bhfilí 1200–1650* (Dublin, Clóchomhar, 1984).

Ó Carragáin, Éamonn, 'Crucifixion as Annunciation: The Relation of *The Dream of the Rood* to the Liturgy Reconsidered', *English Studies*, lxiii (1982), 487–505.

—— 'Rome Pilgrimage, Roman Liturgy, and the Ruthwell Cross', *Akten des XII. Internationalen Kongresses für Christliche Archäologie* (Münster, Aschendorff, 1995), 630–9.

O'Dwyer, Peter, *Célí Dé: Spiritual Reform in Ireland 750–900*, 2nd edn (Dublin, Tailliura, 1981).

—— 'An Mhaighdean Mhuire agus an Nua-Spioradáltacht', in *An Léann Eaglasta in Éirinn 1000–1200*, ed. Martin McNamara (Dublin, Clóchomhar, 1982), 70–6.

—— *Mary: A History of Devotion in Ireland* (Dublin, Four Courts, 1988).

Ogilvy, J. D. A., *Books Known to the English 597–1066* (Cambridge, Mass., Medieval Academy of America, 1967).

Ó Laoghaire, Diarmuid, 'Mary in Irish Spirituality', in *Irish Spirituality*, ed. Michael Maher (Dublin, Veritas, 1981).

O'Loughlin, Thomas, 'The Cult of Mary within the Structures of Human Time: A Reading of Some Early Mediaeval Irish Martyrologies', *Maria*, iii/2 (2003), 135–69.

Ó Macháin, Pádraig, 'Job's Gold in Medieval Ireland', *Notes and Queries*, ccxxxvii (1992), 265–7.

Opie, Iona and Peter, *The Oxford Dictionary of Nursery Rhymes* (Oxford, Clarendon, 1951).

Origo, Iris, *The Merchant of Prato* (London, Cape, 1957).

Oroz Arizcuren, F. J. (ed.), *La lírica religiosa en la literatura provenzal antigua* (Pamplona, Príncipe de Viana, 1972).

O'Sullivan, Anne and Ó Riain, Pádraig (eds), *Poems on Marcher Lords* (London, ITS, 1987).

Owst, G. R., *Literature and Pulpit in Medieval England*, 2nd edn (Oxford, Blackwell, 1961).

Parkes, M. B., 'The Palaeography of the Parker Manuscript of the *Chronicle*', *Anglo-Saxon England*, v (1976), 149–71.

Partridge, Angela, *Caoineadh na dTrí Muire* (Dublin, Clóchomhar, 1983).

Pevsner, Nikolaus, *The Buildings of England: Bedfordshire and the County of Huntingdon and Peterborough* (Harmondsworth, Penguin, 1968).

Pevsner, Nikolaus and Metcalf, Priscilla, *The Cathedrals of England: Midland, Eastern, and Northern England* (Harmondsworth, Penguin, 1985).

Poppe, Erich, 'The Early Modern Irish Version of Beves of Hamtoun', *Cambridge Medieval Celtic Studies*, xxiii (1992), 77–98.

Purtle, Carol, *The Marian Paintings of Jan van Eyck* (Princeton, Princeton University Press, 1982).

Raby, F. J. E, *A History of Christian-Latin Poetry*, 2nd edn (Oxford, Clarendon, 1953).

—— (ed.), *The Oxford Book of Medieval Latin Verse* (Oxford, Clarendon, 1959).

Rauschen, Gerhard, (ed.), *Die Legende Karls des Grossen* (Leipzig, Gesellschaft für reinische Geschichtskunde, 1890).

Réau, Louis, *Iconographie de l'art chrétien* (Paris, Presses universitaires de France, 1955–9).

Reed, Teresa, *Shadows of Mary* (Cardiff, University of Wales Press, 2003).

Reiners, Ludwig (ed.), *Die ewige Brunnen*, 2nd edn

(München, Beck, 1959).

Reinsch, Robert (ed.), *Die Pseudo-Evangelien von Jesu und Maria's Kindheit in der romanischen und germanischen Literatur* (Halle, Niemeyer, 1879).

Richards, W. Leslie (ed.), *Gwaith Dafydd Llwyd o Fathafarn* (Cardiff, Gwasg Prifysgol Cymru, 1964).

Rigg, A. G. and Wieland, G. R., 'A Canterbury Classbook of the Mid-Eleventh Century', *Anglo-Saxon England*, iv (1975), 113–30.

Riou, Y.-F., 'Quelques aspects de la tradition manuscrite des *Carmina* d'Eugène de Tolède', *Revue d'histoire des textes*, ii (1972), 11–44.

Ritchie, W. Tod (ed.), *The Bannatyne Manuscript* (Edinburgh, Blackwood, 1928–34).

Roberts, Brynley F. (ed.), *Gwassanaeth Meir* (Cardiff, Gwasg Prifysgol Cymru, 1961).

Roberts, E. Stanton (ed.), *Llanstephan MS 6* (Cardiff, University of Wales Guild of Graduates, 1916).

Roberts, Thomas, of Bangor (ed.), *Gwaith Dafydd ab Edmwnd* (Bangor, Jarvis and Foster, 1914).

Roberts, Thomas, of Wrexham (ed.), *The Poetical Works of Dafydd Nanmor* (Cardiff, University of Wales Press, 1923).

Robertson, Elizabeth, 'Savoring "Scientia"', in *A Companion to 'Ancrene Wisse'*, ed. Yoko Wada (Cambridge, Brewer, 2003), 113–44.

Rodríguez-Puértolas, Julio, *Fray Iñigo de Mendoza y sus 'Coplas de Vita Christi'* (Madrid, Gredos, 1968).

Rogers, N. J., 'The Boulogne Hours: An Addition to York Art', *The Edam Newsletter*, vi (1983–4), 38.

Routh, Pauline, *Medieval Effigial Alabaster Tombs in Yorkshire* (Ipswich, 1976).

Routh, Pauline and Knowles, Richard, *The Medieval Monuments of Harewood* (Wakefield, Wakefield Historical Society, 1983).

Rowland, Jenny, *Early Welsh Saga Poetry* (Cambridge, Brewer, 1990).

Rowlands, E. I. (ed.), *Gwaith Lewys Môn* (Cardiff, Gwasg Prifysgol Cymru, 1975).

Ruddock, G. E., 'Siôn Cent', in *A Guide to Welsh Literature*, ed. A. O. H. Jarman and G. R. Hughes, ii (Swansea, Christopher Davies, 1979), 169–88.

Salu, Mary (tr.), *Ancrene Riwle* (London, Burns & Oates, 1955).

Salzer, Anselm, *Die Sinnbilder und Beiwörte Mariens* (Linz, Feichtinger, 1886–94).

Santob de Carrión, *Proverbios morales* (Cambridge, Cambridge University Press, 1947).

Sayce, Olive (ed.), *Poets of the Minnesang* (Oxford, Clarendon, 1967).

Schiller, Gertrud, *Iconography of Christian Art* (London, Lund Humphries, 1971–2).

Schmidt, Leopold, *Die Volkerzählung: Märchen, Sage, Legende* (Berlin, Schmidt, 1957).

Silverstein, Theodore (ed.), *Medieval English Lyrics* (London, Arnold, 1971).

Sims-Williams, Patrick, *Religion and Literature in Western England 600–800* (Cambridge, Cambridge University Press, 1990).

Singer, Isaac Bashevis, *The Manor* (Harmondsworth, Penguin, 1975).

Sisam, Celia and Kenneth (eds), *The Oxford Book of Medieval English Verse* (Oxford, Clarendon, 1970).

Southern, R. W., *The Making of the Middle Ages* (London, Hutchinson, 1953).

—— *St Anselm and His Biographer* (Cambridge, Cambridge University Press, 1963).

—— *Medieval Humanism* (Oxford, Blackwell, 1970).

Sparrow, John and Perosa, Alessandro (eds), *Renaissance Latin Verse* (London, Duckworth, 1979).

Spector, Stephen (ed.), *The N-Town Play*, EETS, s.s. 11–12 (Oxford, Oxford University Press, 1991).

Stamm, Christian, *Mariologia* (Paderborniae, Junfermann, 1881).

Stanley, E. G., *A Collection of Papers* (Toronto, PIMS, 1987).

Stevenson, W. H. (ed.), *Asser's Life of King Alfred* (Oxford, Clarendon, 1904).

Stokes, Whitley (ed.), *The Life of St Meriasek* (London, Trübner, 1872).

Swanton, M. J. (ed.), *The Dream of the Rood* (Manchester, Manchester University Press, 1970).

Szövérffy, Josef, *Die Annalen der lateinischen Hymnendichtung* (Berlin, Schmidt, 1964–).

Tait, Clodagh, 'Art and the Cult of the Virgin Mary in Ireland, c.1500–1660', in *Art and Devotion in Late Medieval Ireland*, ed. Rachel Moss, Colmán Ó Clabaigh, and Salvador Ryan (Dublin, Four Courts, 2006), 163–83.

Talbot, C. H. (ed.), *The Life of Christina of Markyate* (Oxford, Clarendon, 1959).

Tschochner, F., 'Gürtel Mariae', *Marienlexikon*, iii (1991), 54.

Thompson, Stith, *Motif-Index of Folk Literature* (Copenhagen, Rosenkilde and Bagger, 1955–8).

Trens, Mañuel, *María: Iconografía de la Virgen en el arte español* (Madrid, Plus Ultra, 1947).

Tristram, E. W., *English Wall Painting of the Fourteenth Century* (London, RKP, 1955).

Tubach, F. C., *Index Exemplorum* (Helsinki, Suomalainen Tiëdeakatemia 1969).

van der Waal, H. (ed.), *Iconclass* (Amsterdam, North Holland, 1973–85).

van Os, H. W., *Marias Demut und Verherrlichung in der Sienesischen Malerei 1300–1450* (The Hague, Ministerie van Cultuur, 1969).

Vendryes, Joseph, 'Le Miracle de la moisson en Galles', *Académie des Inscriptions: Comptes rendus* (1948), 64–76.

—— *Lexique étymologique de l'ancien irlandais: Lettre B* (Paris, CRNS, 1981).

Vollmer, Friedrich (ed.), *Eugenii Toletani episcopi carmina* (Berolini, Weidmann, 1905).

von der Leyen, Friedrich (ed.), *Deutsche Dichtung des Mittelalters* (Frankfurt, Insel, 1962).

Wall, Carolyn, 'The Apocryphal and Historical Backgrounds of "The Appearance of Our Lady to Thomas"', *Medieval Studies*, xxxii (1970), 172–92.

Wall, J. C., *Mediaeval Wall Paintings* (London, Talbot, 1914).

Walther, Hans (ed.), *Lateinischer Sprichwörter und Sentenzen des Mittelalters* (Göttingen, 1963–7).

Weiss, Adolf, 'Die Himmelaufnahme Mariens am Strass-burger Münster', *Die Münster*, iv (1951), 12–18.

Westlake, H. F., *Westminster Abbey* (London, Allen, 1923).

Wesle, Carle (ed.), *Das Rolandsleid des Pfaffen Konrad* (Tübingen, Niemeyer, 1967).

Whitelock, Dorothy (ed.), *English Historical Documents c.500–1042*, 2nd edn (London, Eyre Methuen, 1979).

Willard, Rudolph, 'On Blicking Homily XIII', *Review of English Studies*, xii (1936), 1–17.

Williams, Glanmor, *The Welsh Church from Conquest to Reformation* (Cardiff, University of Wales Press, 1962).

Williams, G. J., 'Cywyddau ac Awdlau Pen-Rhys', *Efrydiau Catholig*, v (1951), 40–5.

Williams, Ifor, 'Cywydd Cyfrinach Rhys Goch Eryri', *Bulletin of the Board of Celtic Studies*, i (1921–3), 43–50.

—— 'Ave, Eva', *Bulletin of the Board of Celtic Studies*, i (1921–3), 334.

—— (ed.), *Casgliad o Waith Ieuan Deulwyn* (Bangor, Jarvis and Foster, 1909).

—— (ed.), *Gwyneddon 3* (Cardiff, Gwasg Prifysgol Cymru, 1931).

—— (ed.), *Canu Llywarch Hen* (Cardiff, Gwasg Prifysgol Cymru, 1935).

—— and Roberts, Thomas (eds), *Cywyddau Dafydd ap Gwilym a'i Gyfoeswyr*, 2nd edn (Cardiff, Gwasg Prifysgol Cymru, 1935).

Williams, J. E. Caerwyn, 'Beirdd y Tywysogion: Arolwg', *Llên Cymru*, xi (1970–1), 3–94.

—— *Canu Crefyddol y Gogynfeirdd* (Swansea, Coleg y Brifysgol, 1977).

Williams, J. Ll. and Williams, Ifor (eds), *Gwaith Guto'r Glyn* (Cardiff, Gwasg Prifysgol Cymru, 1939).

Williams, N. J. A. (ed.), *The Poems of Giolla Brighde Mac Con Midhe* (London, ITS, 1980).

Williamson, W. W., 'Saints on Norfolk Rood Screens and Pulpits', *Norfolk Archaeology*, xxxi (1955–7), 299–346.

Wilmart, André, *Auteurs spirituels et textes dévots* (Paris, Bloud et Gay, 1932).

Wilson, R. M., 'The Contents of the Mediaeval Library', in

The English Library before 1700, ed. Francis Wormald and C. E. Wright (London, 1958), 85–111.

Woolf, Rosemary, *The English Religious Lyric in the Middle Ages* (Oxford, Clarendon, 1968).

—— *The English Mystery Plays* (London, RKP, 1972).

Wormald, Francis, 'The Monastic Library', in *The English Library before 1700*, ed. Francis Wormald and C. E. Wright (London, Athlone, 1958), 15–31.

Wormald, Patrick, 'The Age of Bede and Æthelbald', in *The Anglo-Saxons*, ed. James Campbell (Oxford, Phaidon, 1982), 70–100.

Wright, C. D., *The Irish Tradition in Old English Literature* (Cambridge, Cambridge University Press, 1993).

Wright, Neil, 'The *Hisperica Famina* and Caelius Sedulius', *Cambridge Medieval Celtic Studies*, iv (1982), 61–76.

Index

CPSIA information can be obtained
at www.ICGtesting.com
Printed in the USA
BVOW08s2053280118
506565BV00001B/50/P